# PRAISE FOR...
## *The Corporate Introvert:*
## *How to Lead and Thrive with Confidence*

"Steve's ability to articulate introversion in a positive light is awesome! He has a way of helping you see how you can capitalize on your talents so that you can achieve what you want in the workplace and in life."
**AMY DIX,**
**Two-Time Bestselling Author, Podcast Host of** *Happiest Places to Work*

"Steve Friedman is a compassionate and thoughtful author who offers an inspiring read that also serves as an empowering desktop reference book. It's just what new and aspiring leaders are searching for to lead in authentic ways."
**NORMA HOLLIS,**
**Authenticity Coach, NormaHollis.com**

"This book is a godsend to introverts. With an eye for the landmines that introverts encounter in the corporate world, Steve Friedman takes you gently by the arm and provides you with tools of how to navigate the territory of what it's like to be an introvert in an extroverted world. Most importantly, Friedman encourages us to confront what can be challenges for introverts – meetings, cocktail hours, presentations – with courage, self-compassion and by staying true to ourselves. What a relief to know that as introverts, we can accept ourselves just as we are and recognize that we have gifts and talents to bring to this extroverted world!"
**KAREN BLUTH, PhD,**
**Author of** *The Self-Compassionate Teen,*
**University of North Carolina, Chapel Hill**

"Steve Friedman has written a must-read for any introvert who is tired of compromising who they are at work and wants to thrive by being themselves."
**THEA OROZCO,**
**Author of *The Introvert's Guide to the Workplace***

"Just the right mix of stories, data, models and motivation to energize introverts to lead with confidence."
**JENNIFER B. KAHNWEILER, PhD,**
**Author of *Creating Introvert-Friendly Workplaces***

"This is a much-needed book for introverts in the workplace. There is not just information for introverts in the corporate world, but each chapter also has action steps that can boost personal strengths."
**Dr. TY BELKNAP,**
**Author of *Leadership for Introverts: The Power of Quiet Influence***

"I absolutely resonate with this book and its importance in helping those in the corporate world appreciate the gifts that come with being introverted. I spent years posting 'Do Not Disturb' signs outside my office before I understood why I found interruptions so distracting. Now I embrace being an introvert and all the value it brings to my life. I highly recommend this insightful book!"
**STEPHANIE CHANDLER,**
**Author and CEO, NonfictionAuthorsAssociation.com**

"Friedman presents a compelling case for introverts to lead, and then he shows us how to do it our way!"
**JENNIFER GRANNEMAN,**
**Founder of *Introvert, Dear***

"*The Corporate Introvert* guides us through the work of developing our authentic style and empowers us to lead with confidence."
**KIM MENINGER,**
**Executive Coach & Consultant, Your Career Success**

"Pairing his 30 years of corporate leadership with his belief in the power of introverts, Friedman guides readers down a path of self-discovery in finding their natural leadership style. This empowering book shows us how to nourish our roots so we can lead -- and thrive -- with our unique introverted strengths."

**MATTHEW POLLARD,**
**Author of the bestselling *Introvert's Edge Series***

"As an introvert, navigating the corporate world can be daunting - how can you thrive without getting burnt out or losing who you are. So finding an informative guide drawn from Friedman's corporate experience that offers answers and ideas for introverts is a welcomed and much-needed resource."

**HANNAH STAINER,**
***Psykhe Mental Wellbeing* Podcast**

"Steve's experience navigating introversion in a corporate world is insightful and comes from first-hand experience and research. So many great tips that will raise your comfort and confidence at work."

**JETTE STUBBS,**
**Career & Business Coach, *Happy Career Formula* Podcast**

"A refreshingly discerning look at a consistently misunderstood subject. Valuable for introverts to help them build and take pride in their unique strengths. Priceless for extroverts in leadership positions because it offers insight on how to better understand the introverts on their team and how to permit those skills to shine in a way that lets both the individual and organization truly thrive."

**HANNA HASI-KELCHNER,**
**Producer and Host of *Business Confidential Now***

# THE
# CORPORATE
# INTROVERT

## HOW TO LEAD AND THRIVE
## WITH CONFIDENCE

STEVE FRIEDMAN

# The Corporate Introvert

How to Lead and Thrive with Confidence

Steve Friedman

Peavine Press, LLC
Houston, Texas

Publisher: Peavine Press, LLC

Houston, Texas USA


www.BeyondIntroversion.com/tci-landing-page

BeyondIntroversion@gmail.com


ISBN: 978-1-7342211-2-1 (ebook), 978-1-7342211-4-5 (paper), 978-1-7342211-5-2 (hard)

Library of Congress Catalog Number: 2021916051

FREE BONUS – Complimentary worksheets available at www.BeyondIntroversion.com/tci-landing-page

# CONTENTS

# DEDICATION

To my family, who have taught me the power of being authentic.

To our oldest, Gwendolyn, who teaches me every day to worry a bit less about what everyone else may think and focus more on my own dreams.

To Maddie, who teaches me to be brave in defeating societal norms in pursuit of passion.

To our youngest, Noah, who teaches me to use my strengths and passions in every facet of my life.

And finally, to my magnificent wife, Jennifer, who provided me with a refuge when I struggled and an oasis of love and support when I found my true passion.

Together, you have taught me that only by being the student can you become a better teacher.

*All my love,*
*Steve*

# Preface

# Global Pandemic – Reflecting on Authenticity

In early 2020, the world never imagined enduring the chaos of the COVID-19 pandemic. Yet this crisis forced us all to reevaluate the world as we knew it. Our health, stability, and routines that we had taken for granted were suddenly threatened by a strange intruder. Many claimed that lockdowns were like living in an introvert's world. Yet this only underscored the simplistic view of introversion and its impact on those who are reserved or less enamored with an overly social life. Nevertheless, many people chose to live this period with purpose rather than write off the year with sorrow, if not anger.

Scores of people cherished newfound time with parents, kids, and spouses. People discovered hobbies that were shelved for decades. Not surprisingly, this chaos led many people to reevaluate their life priorities and level of satisfaction.

Often, introverts keep personal and work lives separate. We enjoy our family and private time with a more reflective mindset at home, yet we tend to cover up our true selves at work. We attempt to conform to corporate norms of gregarious socializing, aggressive debating, and excessive self-promotion because that seems to be the model of success.

As COVID-19 fades from the headlines, the same contemplation that helped us adjust to homeschooling, grocery delivery, remote work, and family events by Zoom is sparking introverts to reflect on how work can be more satisfying and rewarding. Whether at home or on the job, the answer often comes back to living authentically – discovering our true strengths, protecting our personal style, and proudly leveraging it to pair happiness with success.

*Steve Friedman*
*July 2021*

# Introduction

*"Nothing can dim the light that shines from within."*
—*Maya Angelou, American poet, memoirist, and civil rights activist (1951-2014)*

Introversion is not a curse but a blessing. Introverts can stop trying to merely survive at work, and instead start embracing our unique talents to lead teams and organizations. More importantly, introverts can do all of this without compromising who we are or exhausting ourselves each day. Introverts can follow our passions, make a difference, and find personal satisfaction at work.

The above assertions may sound strange to many introverts who often feel handcuffed, drained from a day trying to perform within the norms of an extroverted office culture, yet unsure how to bring their true personality and strengths to the workplace. As Jennifer Brown states in her book *How to be an Inclusive Leader*, introverts "don't feel comfortable bringing their whole selves to work."

You may be seeking that magic ingredient to enable you to excel in meetings, be a smooth networker, and lead productive teams, but in order for introverts to contribute our talents and find true joy at work, let's step back and do some groundwork first. Once we explore your strengths and passions, you will be much better prepared and confident to navigate the most challenging circumstances and liberate yourselves from the stigmas that often overwhelm introverts. Let's start by first assessing where you are on your own journey.

## Navigating the 5 Phases of Introversion

Introversion is not a state of being. It is an evolving journey that each of us began long ago. If we continue to travel down this path, we will find the greater peace and tranquility we all seek. Unfortunately for many, this may take a lifetime. The purpose of *The Corporate Introvert* is to provide the tools to accelerate your journey. We all have the capability to learn, to grow, and to thrive with our introversion. Let's first understand the five phases of introversion and where you are on your own path so that you can apply each section of this book to advance your own transformation.

1. **Unaware**: Many of us have known we are different from others since our earliest childhood memories, perhaps nudged outside by parents to play with others when all we really wanted to do was stay home and read or lose ourselves in our hobbies. We may have had a small group of two or three friends, but often wondered why we were tongue-tied at gatherings or never had much confidence as a kid. The term "introversion" is typically not introduced until our late teens or early 20s. This phase is often the longest, especially when we are surrounded by loudness and bravado on TV, social media, and at school and home. Others may have received open support from friends and family to accelerate through this stage. The longer we stay in this phase, the more damage we may suffer to our self-confidence—and the harder it can be to move on.

2. **Uninformed**: As adults, most introverts eventually connect with their introspective label, yet many don't really understand what it means. We assume the stereotypes of "loner," "anti-social," and "hermit" must apply to us. Many confuse shyness with introversion. Others develop such deep scars from decades of fighting societal norms, not to mention their own personal torment, that they consider introversion nearly a death sentence. I wandered in this phase from my early 20s until my mid-40s. BeyondIntroversion.com's informal Facebook poll found many respondents didn't move out of this phase until their 40s or 50s. No one mandates a long stay in this stage. We need to take the lead towards establishing our own peace and tranquility to move on.

3. **Enlightenment**: Most adults eventually do move into this phase prompted, perhaps, by writings like Susan Cain's revolutionary book *Quiet*, a caring friend, a mentor, or a therapist. Others are spurred on by their own sense of curiosity, a mid-life crisis, or other life-changing events. During this stage introverts finally recognize there is nothing "wrong" with them. Everyone in the world is unique. We have plenty of strengths that are just different from our extroverted friends. Rather than thriving in social gatherings, debates, or brainstorming sessions, we often excel with listening, planning, curiosity, and thoughtfulness. Once we realize the value of these traits, which we have hidden for years, it is often as if a veil is lifted and we can see the opportunities that lie ahead. This phase can often be the shortest as we are fueled by optimism, excitement, and determination.

4. **Contentment**: Though our learning and growth in the Enlightenment phase should never end, we can reach a point of contentment. We may finally embrace our introversion—indeed, our true selves—for the first time. We are at peace

alone. We understand how to manage our energy levels to continue to perform during long days. We are confident in who we are and understand that others will benefit from hearing our perspectives and feeling our warmth, both at work and at home. This is a good place to be; a tranquil and satisfying spot.

5. **Flourishing Introvert**: Many introverts, fueled by the power of their own strengths and previously stifled ambitions, now seek to put their personality to work for them. They not only champion their own introversion to pursue dreams once thought unattainable, but they also share in the hope of short-circuiting this long journey for others. They may apply their bolstered confidence and style by using their introspective traits to teach, create artistically, write, or somehow share their wonderful talents that have been bottled up for so long. Not everyone seeks to enter this phase. For those introverts who do, a dose of patience and self-compassion goes a long way as you stretch your comfort zone and flourish.

Where are you today on your journey? What is holding you back from your next phase?

Regardless of which phase you are in now, this book will help you accelerate your journey. You will learn to celebrate your differences and travel your own path. The world needs you and your gifts, and you need to find the confidence and peace you seek and deserve.

## Shifting Your Mindset

What would it be like to be comfortable at work? To be energized at the end of the day? To make a difference every day—in your own skin? To be respected and recognized by your peers?

Envision releasing your true personality to shine. Can you picture yourself confident and happy at work and at home?

The term "superpowers" connotates comic strip stars with outlandish strengths and skills that they wield for good. The term is used a lot these days, but it's the best term to aptly describe the talents, mindsets, and passions which introverts hold. Like many on-screen avengers, we may not even know the talents we have, much less how to use them. This is a key objective of this book. Your superpowers are strengths that already exist within you. It will take exploration and practice to utilize them as superpowers, but embracing these muscles is the key to conquering some of your greatest fears.

It is time for introverts and leaders alike to change society's long-held beliefs. With a renewed mindset, you can build an authentic life full of confidence, success, and pride. Let's analyze three such truths:

1.  Introversion is a force, not an obstacle.

2.  Leadership is an approach, not a position.

3.  Work success comes from authenticity, not at its expense.

Those who see the opportunity to contest societal norms and explore these truths will be justly rewarded. So let's get started.

## Introversion is a Force

Let's first unpack a term that you have likely wrestled with much of your life: introversion. When you hear "introversion," do you think of words like *anti-social, low self-esteem, different, quiet,* or even *loner* or *not normal?* It's fair to have those notions. Many of these terms filled our playgrounds and even our homes. They brought sadness and insecurities. Too many are still listed in dictionaries and thesauruses today. But these are terms of the past. The modern world welcomes diversity and invites different perspectives and styles. The time is ripe for us to exert our strengths.

Introversion does not mean "anti-social." Many introverts thoroughly enjoy time with family and friends. But at the end of a long day, introverts gravitate toward solo activities like relaxing with a good book or music or exploring other talents through creative hobbies such as writing or art. Conversely, extroverts refuel by spending time with others. A weekend filled with dinners and parties may be the perfect combination for extroverts to unwind and reenergize for their week ahead.

Introversion is merely a label to describe your comfort zone and the skills with which you operate. Introversion is every bit as glorious as extroversion. Yet damage is done to our self-image when either term is characterized as a flaw or a trait that must be corrected. Everyone's personality exists along the introversion/ extroversion continuum and each of us moves along that range depending on specific circumstances, whether at work meetings or during playtime with our kids. We are not simply introverts or extroverts, but complex individuals filled with strengths, curiosities, aspirations, and fears. I will refer to "introverts" throughout this book in recognition of our common talents and tendencies. We will discover how to identify and reinforce your own personality strengths and how to utilize them in various situations to bring about confidence and pride.

A revolution has begun in the twenty-first century. It is time to truly understand introversion: the stereotypes, the tendencies, the strengths, and talents it provides. Instead of fighting the label, how can we embrace it and use this knowledge to thrive? We will explore each of these areas as they relate to us as individuals, and then we will apply them to the work environment.

## Leadership is an Approach

Do you consider yourself a leader at work? This term also has an antiquated definition. You may not be a supervisor or manager of people at this point, but we can all be leaders. After all, the best leaders show vision, empathy, teamwork, and courage—regardless of whether or not they actually manage others. In fact, everyone has the capacity to be a role model. Each organization desperately needs a leader's characteristics in order to effectively deliver a product or service to their customers. Yet many supervisors don't exhibit these traits, often overcome by ego, power, greed, or ignorance. Regardless of position, there are far too many employees who either lack the confidence or are not provided the support to show the leadership that is within them.

Many extroverts—and plenty of introverts as well—may be skeptical of our qualifications to be great leaders, but I'm proud to say that you hold the key. Common introvert strengths like listening, learning, resilience, and empathy are traits often found in exceptional leaders. The challenge is for you to discover these strengths and the mindset to use them in various situations to be that leader. This is not a heart-wrenching story, but one of resolve and triumph! You will unlock the leadership within you in the pages ahead.

## Work Success Comes from Authenticity

Our society has conditioned us to believe that work is, well, work. We endure the drudgery of the weekdays in hopes of recuperation and distraction over the weekend. Thus, many introverts suspect the anxiety and discomforts of work are to be expected. However, job satisfaction, pride, and happiness are not unreasonable expectations at work. You will find joy at work as you succeed by being who you are, not in spite of it. I have lived this experience.

Spurred on by my drive to succeed and provide for my family, I aimed high in my career. For years I donned a mask so others wouldn't see my fears and anxiety. I pretended to be more like others: outgoing, energetic, and a relentless ladder-climber. Yet I struggled to survive under the pressure to conform to the prevailing corporate culture and my own lofty expectations. I was drained at the end of each day. Many of you may have similar stories, in desperate need of the same magic formula for which I was searching.

Finally, late in my career, my relentless need to succeed and provide for my family became overwhelming, jeopardizing my health and my family bonds. At rock bottom, I challenged the paradigm that I must choose between work success and happiness. I was determined to have both. During my quest, I found the courage to tackle my most important project: me. I finally learned about myself – my reserved nature, my strengths, my fears, my priorities. I didn't change myself; I just learned how to embrace and use my natural talents.

I began to reassess my leadership style. Rather than follow others, I fortified my own strengths and style with confidence and began to proactively manage in a truly authentic way. Suddenly, I began enjoying my job a lot more because I was using my energy to apply my talents rather than to conceal my genuine strengths. My teams became more cohesive and successful as a result.

During my career I led a variety of trading, distribution, and supply teams in head office, field locations, and overseas. I collected many scrapes and painful lessons along the way. However, once I shed the mask I'd worn for decades and embraced my true self, I discovered career success does not have to pair with personal destruction.

## My Mission

After a frustrating childhood and decades as a conflicted adult, my own journey provides me the opportunity to share stories and strengths through books and online communities. I hope to be a catalyst for your own journey toward contentment and flourishing.

I'm not a therapist or life coach, but I am a 30-year veteran of the corporate world and a lifelong introvert who has struggled, survived, learned, succeeded beyond my wildest dreams, and now champions introversion for myself and advocates for others.

I've met so many people who are going through their own challenges at home and work. This book is intended to provide valuable guidance to leverage your strengths, mindset, and growth to conquer typically challenging situations for introverts such as communications, meetings, networking, and team leadership so that you may find comfort and confidence in your own style.

## Our Journey

Throughout this book I will share personal stories as well as those from other introverts who are famous writers, leaders, and public figures, along with everyday people paving their own path. I've included testimonials from our introvert community's petition to update harmful definitions of introversion. Their stories are raw and thought provoking. Sprinkled in the discussion will be statistics from my Introvert Talent and Leadership quizzes, which have tapped over a thousand introverts to provide insights and broad perspectives to our journey. Links to these quizzes and the associated learning materials are included in the book, along with links to free worksheets that accompany many of the chapters.

Throughout *The Corporate Introvert* we will lean on the analogy of a tree. Trees can grow strong and expansive, but they require a vast root system, continuous nourishment, a supportive environment, and a dose of patience. Our personal journey is much the same. After we lay the groundwork by demystifying introversion, we will begin building a strong tree, a tree that uses nutrients to grow and flourish in a field of challenges and opportunities:

- The first section of *The Corporate Introvert*, "Building Your Roots," serves to help you discover your introvert talents, values, and mindset—the essential nutrients for personal and professional growth along your journey. When you bundle these roots together, you possess your own superpowers that prepare you to reach for the sky.

- Section two, "Flexing Your Branches," guides you to apply your strong foundation to tackle a variety of typical work obstacles including uncertainty, communication, meetings, and networking so you can confidently get your voice heard in meeting rooms and social gatherings.

- Section three, "Reaching for the Sky," challenges you to navigate your environment and workplace dynamics to nurture your superpowers for good.

- Section four, "Blossoming Leader," drives managers to share their superpowers and confidence as seedlings to help others grow and flourish.

Each chapter begins with a quote from a well-known introvert and ends with actions to help you retain key points and begin to put them into practice.

Most references and stories best apply to medium- and large-sized companies, though lessons abound for small business owners and freelancers as well. Whether you are a seasoned veteran, a green supervisor, or an aspiring leader, this is a personal journey of discovery. It's about exploring how you can use the authentic strengths that reside within you. This book is about finding your leadership as an introvert. By the end of this quest, you will proudly exclaim your introversion and successfully manage challenging situations **your way**. Welcome to your exciting and empowering journey!

## ACTIONS:

1. What phase of introversion are you currently in?
2. What is holding you back from the next phase in your journey? Brainstorm a list of obstacles, small and large.
3. Open your mind and be prepared to change your approach to everything.

## *The Corporate Introvert* – **Accompanying Worksheets**

Free Worksheets accompany most chapters so you can record your strengths, values, and passions and develop your own plan to apply your talents to become a confident and authentic leader.

https://www.BeyondIntroversion.com/tci-landing-page

Chapter One

# INTROVERSION 101:
# Knowledge is Power

*"Our culture made a virtue of living only as extroverts.*
*We discouraged the inner journey, the quest for a center.*
*So we lost our center and have to find it again."*
—*Anaïs Nin, French Cuban American diarist and essayist*
*(1903-1977)*

What is introversion? Are there degrees of introversion? Can we overcome it?

Depending on where you are on your introversion journey, you may find introversion a novel concept. Perhaps you have set the idea aside without much consideration, or maybe you are exploring how to turn this label into an advantage. It helps to gain some perspective regarding introversion, so you can challenge old definitions. Once equipped with facts, you can debunk stereotypes, reveal true strengths, and figure out how to use those superpowers to be stronger. Fortunately, the momentum of change in society is creating an atmosphere of transformation for introverts.

## The Introvert Revolution

What has ushered in this era of change, opening a new world for introverts? Three recent developments have made headlines over the past couple of decades:

1. **Diversity & Inclusion Makes Dramatic Advancements:** Though broad inclusion in American society has been slow and painful for decades, the 1990s and early 2000s not only saw progress regarding the inclusion of African Americans and women in the workplace, but also a greater appreciation for other differences such as LGBTQ+ and gender identities, as well as more positive inclusion of Native Americans and immigrants in the American workforce. More diverse work groups functioning together certainly helps people understand, appreciate, and become more comfortable with each other. Society is recognizing that not only do people have more in common than our differences, but also that these differences are strengths that help improve society, business decisions, and places of learning.

   It is against this backdrop that the introversion-extroversion spectrum has come under the microscope in the past ten years, resulting in more openminded attitudes. Schools, workplaces, and families are beginning to change their understanding of introversion. Introversion is no longer seen merely as the antithesis of extroversion. It is simply another perspective which, if harnessed, can provide a foundation for success and happiness for the introvert while making our communities better.

2. **Brain Chemistry Shapes Persona:** Recent research has determined that dopamine and acetylcholine have a significant impact on the different actions and behavior of introverts

and extroverts.[1] Everyone has the same amount of dopamine and acetylcholine in their bodies. Both provide a feeling of happiness to the individual. So why do introvert and extroverts have such different personalities?

Extroverts have more dopamine receptors than introverts. They also have a high tolerance for dopamine, so they end up craving it in order to get enough to satiate the receptors. Dopamine is released into the brain from the expectation of and actual activities with external stimuli like socializing, talking, and adventure. When dopamine is released, it travels on the short dopamine highway; thus, there is a brief time span between stimulus and reward.

Introverts, however, crave acetylcholine just as extroverts need dopamine. Acetylcholine is released when we are calm, quiet, and introspective in thought. Thus, the more we engage in these traditionally introverted strong suits, the greater sense of contentment we receive. When acetylcholine is released, it travels on a much longer acetylcholine highway to frontal lobes of the brain where empathy, self-reflection, emotions, planning, self-talk, and memories are stored. Because this highway is quite a bit longer than for dopamine, introverts tend to take more time to process, ponder, think, and act. That contributes to why introverts are typically less spontaneous or comfortable making rapid decisions.

This information enables introverts to explain personality differences with science rather than attributing one's preference for solitude as anti-social behavior or mere awkwardness, thus contributing to a person's enlightenment and growth.

3. **Mental Health Dialogue Becomes More Common:** Most of us are accustomed to getting an annual physical exam and

seeking a doctor's opinion when we need comfort and cures. Recently, these same avenues for mental health have become less taboo. Stress, anxiety, and depression are common with today's life pressures. It is becoming acceptable to seek professional help to address episodic problems, such as stress resulting from traumatic events. Even more importantly, just as we have primary care physicians, more people are engaging therapists on an ongoing basis to make sense of complex issues and develop healthier coping skills[2].

While personality traits have a distinct genetic origin, it is widely understood that family upbringing and traumatic events can magnify such traits.[3] Melanie O. shares "I'm an introvert, and it's frustrating living in a society where extroverts are worshipped while introverts are misunderstood, ostracized, and negatively stereotyped." The parent who embraces their child's reserved nature and love of books provides a vastly different nurturing environment than the parent who insists something is wrong with their child and schedules a stream of play dates. School bullying or parental name-calling also tend to detract from kids' self-awareness and level of confidence. People such as teachers, clergy, or camp counselors can impact a child's self-image.

As adults, we lean on our maturity and wisdom to minimize the impact of childhood events, but these bruises do not disappear overnight. This is especially hard for introverts who reflect often, but don't always confide in even their closest friends or spouses. Today's mainstreaming of mental health is helping to better understand formative and traumatic events, freeing us to embrace ourselves and use our strengths to be happier and more successful. Therapists can provide support by listening and offering time-tested and creative ideas that we can use to learn from others and ourselves. It's like our own introverted friend, but we get to skip the chitchat – truly a gift to ourselves.

Do these three recent developments and the more open discussion of personality traits feel revolutionary to you? The answer depends on your personal experiences, but regardless, the transformation is ushering in an exciting time of self-awareness and inclusion that calls for us to understand and embrace our best selves.

## Old Definitions Can Leave Deep Wounds

Carl Jung first coined the term introversion through his work on psychological types during the 1920s. Since then, many definitions and theories have circulated. As terms like introversion became more mainstream in the 1970s and 1980s, they were often defined by what they were not – extroversion. If extroverts were social, gregarious, and energetic, introverts were labeled the opposite: homebodies, aloof, and reclusive. Since extroverts were considered the social norm, introverts–by definition–were considered outcasts.[4]

These stereotypes were fed by misunderstanding. This is easy to trace. People interpreted this branding often through the lens of the extroverted society that dominates American culture–on TV and in movies, and throughout our schools and work institutions. As kids from that era grew up, few TV shows depicted the introspective thinker and even fewer schools or businesses favored the quiet listener. The rewards went to the loudest, brashest, and most outgoing. Jolene T. of New Zealand shares: "In my life I have been labeled with words that heavily imply there is something inherently wrong with me simply because I need time alone to recharge."

Extroverts latched onto these definitions, but introverts were also complicit, accepting these definitions to their own detriment. Even in the late twentieth century, information about the more practical definitions of introversion was scant for the general public. Meanwhile, discomfort, misunderstanding, and bullying all drew the introvert closer to their introspective core. This hardly created a strong and knowledgeable self-advocate prepared to debate and refute stereotypes. Instead, it fortified others' perceptions that introverts were lazy, anti-social, and poor communicators. Surely, introverts have a variety of youthful experiences which define each person's level of discomfort and confidence. But without a support network of people or information to dispel all the stereotypes, low self-esteem, shame, and sadness often set in. Many introverts grew up with poor self-confidence, exhibiting a timid nature. Apprehension about competing with extroverts in a more sociable world often led to disappointment and frustration.

However, poor self-esteem is not a genetic trait of introverts. It is a by-product of our environment and the lack of encouragement to recognize our authenticity during our most formative years. If we learn how to manage various situations through our own innate strengths, suddenly the pervasive discomfort many endure can disappear and our mindset shifts from coping with the burden of introversion to leveraging the strengths of our awesome personality.

## Modern Definition: The Energy Equation

What is the most accurate definition of introversion? Thankfully, the old descriptions are fading away and being replaced by common phrases, such as people who like to be alone or those who get energy from within. While many of us can relate at times to the former definition, we may struggle to interpret the latter.

The Energy Equation is the simplest way to consider introversion. Everyone has a personal battery that gains and spends energy throughout the day. A good night's sleep typically recharges our battery. We gain energy throughout the day by tapping our strengths and performing tasks we enjoy. We spend energy by performing tasks that may be difficult or contentious.

## The Energy Equation

$$\text{Battery Level} = E_g - E_s$$
**(Energy gained less Energy spent)**

At the end of a long workweek, extroverts often line up dinners and social events to wind down and reenergize. Introverts, on the other hand, may gain energy through hobbies such as reading or crafts, as well as family time. Our Introvert Talent Survey revealed that 68% of introverts enjoy a variety of creative hobbies such as music, art, writing, woodwork, or sewing to wind down, while only 3% indicate they like to hang out with friends in their spare time.

Conversely, introverts may deplete their energy in long meetings, debates, presentations, or cocktail hours. Extroverts often drain their batteries when they are alone for too long.

Also consider those actions that are turbo-boosters: activities which help you recharge quickly so you can make the most of a short break to rekindle your energy. These tend to be our favorite hobbies or work tasks that use our innate strengths.

Your days are likely made up of a wide variety of undertakings in which you gain and spend energy. It is important to mentally monitor your battery's energy gauge. No one should spend the day constantly draining their battery only to refill once they're home. That's a stressful equation that leads to underperformance as the battery approaches empty. Carve out opportunities to recharge during the day. Go for a walk, read a few pages, or treat yourself to lunch alone. Plan your most important meetings when you expect to have high energy, often in the morning or after a recharging break. Scatter more enjoyable work tasks like project planning or meeting preparation in between more stressful activities. This will help you remain active and positive and avoid crashing on the couch from exhaustion at the end of the day.

You can follow this same guidance outside of work. Before a social outing, spend time alone, perhaps reading, journaling, listening to music, or painting. As you sense your energy drop during social events, take a walk, help the organizer with dishes, or escape to the bathroom for a moment of peace and quiet. Aim to call it a night before a fully drained battery leaves you in a foul mood, ready to bolt for the door without the slightest of farewells.

Rebecca W. of Houston notes: "The recharging throughout the day is finally happening. I'm learning to listen to my body... I'm trying to be present [and] enjoy the sunshine." Renee F. of Orlando adds: "I have realized how much I love my 'me' time. It gives me a chance to unwind and recharge." Proactive management of your Energy Equation will make your days more productive and your evenings more enjoyable.

## Introversion and Shyness Are Not the Same

Many people, including the shy and the introverted, often use these terms interchangeably. Many introverts are shy, yet others are not.

Contrary to introversion, shyness is not genetic but often arises from deep-rooted pain. Westfield, Massachusetts Social Worker/ Therapist Susan Morton defines it as a social anxiety: "People with social anxiety experience intense fear of being in one or more social situations. [They] avoid social situations altogether, to avoid experiencing the anxiety [it] create[s] for the person."

Many children endured such social situations when they were teased and bullied for the way they looked, the clothes they wore, their quirkiness, or their inability to chitchat during recess. In other cases, they may simply forget a line of a poem they are reciting in class, or they may miss a pop fly in gym class, inciting others to laugh at their own expense. They may fumble their words at a lunchtime conversation, only to be ridiculed for not fitting in. Children can do cruel things to boost their young egos, and the resulting embarrassment, agony, and grief can leave an indelible mark.

Yet others may have been fortunate to avoid the bullying, only to receive the same shyness label when schoolmates, teachers, or parents mistook innate introversion for shyness. How many introverts can still hear the words ringing in their ears: "Oh, she's just shy"? We may have misused that moniker ourselves. Labels can stick with us, seemingly becoming immovable objects.

For shy people, it is comforting to remove themselves from the crowds and risky situations. Over the years they may build a protective shield to avoid the pain. They become afraid to speak up for fear of being teased or called names. They try to shrink into the background to avoid the bullies and intimidators.

Years later, those traumatic instances of their childhood and their resultant shyness remain. They are scared that they will forget their work presentation or will fumble their words at a business meeting when seemingly all eyes are upon them. Shy people may shake over the prospect of entering a contentious conversation, one in which they are not equipped to articulate their position. What if they forget the words? What if they stumble and pause with a soliloquy of ums and ahs? People will point and chuckle. And worse yet, others will talk about them behind their back for days. These repercussions are unlikely to happen in the adult world, but they are real fears which often originate during childhood, affecting their performance and self-confidence.

Introverts can definitely relate to these shielding steps–not necessarily because we are afraid but because we have not prepared our materials or mindset for stressful situations, and we likely haven't boosted our energy level before the event. If we are both introverted and shy, we are especially reticent to put ourselves out there. It is important to recognize if you are shy, an introvert, or both.

Introversion is part of our DNA. We cannot "overcome" our introversion. Instead, we do best to embrace our true self, learn how to use our strengths to overcome our apprehensions, and manage our Energy Equation to remain present. While it is equally acceptable to be shy, shyness can be managed by improving self-confidence and self-image through practice of a positive and supportive mindset, all of which we will learn about in the next few chapters.

## The Introversion-Extroversion Continuum

Introversion and extroversion live on a continuum. Few people reside on either extreme–always introverts or extroverts in all situations. Thus, everyone finds themselves at various points on the Introversion-Extroversion Continuum based on specific circumstances.[5] For example, often introverts are especially reserved in big crowds of strangers yet are quite talkative within smaller groups of friends or co-workers. Others are calm and resilient under pressure on topics they know, but need a time-out to assess the situation when an emergency arises. People are scattered all across the continuum, due to varying situations and the specific phase of their own introvert journey.

My Introvert Talent Survey, with over 1,350 respondents, highlights several strong trends. Introverts share many, but not all, personality traits and skills. Clearly, reserved people will land more often on the introversion side while gregarious socialites will sit more soundly on the extroverted end of the spectrum. There is no right or wrong place to be on this continuum. Just recognize that no two people, regardless of a common label of introversion, are alike. For our purposes in this book, I will use the term "introvert" to represent those who have more traits and strengths in common with our definition of introversion.

Despite being considered "odd" or a burden by society in the past, introverts bring distinct skills and unique ways of managing and overcoming hurdles. We suffer when we don't understand who we are and thus can't embrace ourselves, instead comparing ourselves to superficial societal norms. This leads to a sense of being broken or not normal. Instead, it's helpful to recognize that everyone's personality is different. We all have our strengths and challenges. The world needs introverts—shy or not. These qualities themselves are not the problem. It is the torment we and others place upon ourselves and each other that is most dangerous. It's time we give ourselves the gifts of knowledge and acceptance so we can flip the inherent burden into our greatest advantage.

## ACTIONS:

1. Consider the Energy Equation. What work, family, or social activities do you do that will build your energy? Which are your turbo boosters? Write these down for reference in Section II.

2. Do you prefer your alone time or are you truly afraid to speak in public? Understanding whether or not you are shy will help you address your introversion and shyness in unique ways.

3. Recognize where on the Introversion-Extroversion Continuum you may reside in different circumstances throughout your day.

## SECTION I:

# BUILDING YOUR ROOTS

Everyone enjoys the beauty and magnificence of trees in the yard, neighborhood, and along their travels. Many trees grow full and tall, adorned with a wide variety of colorful leaves. However, the health of the tree is determined mainly below the surface. Nutrients are largely received not through its branches or leaves, but by water and minerals absorbed through an expansive root system. Much the same can be said about ourselves and our confidence and success at work. We can't jump forward yet and try to improve our networking or meeting performance without addressing our root system. What is our personal root system and how can we nourish it?

In Section I we will cover two types of roots in chapters two and three: talents and values. These are the backbone of the tree ecology. These roots are critical to a tree's health. Without nourishment they will die. Thus, to blossom as a confident employee and inspiring leader, we need to continually nourish these roots with a positive attitude and high energy, the subject of chapters four and five. As we do that, these roots will grow to form a strong trunk that represents our superpowers, poised to deliver confidence, success, and joy throughout our work system.

## The Introvert Talent Quiz

Explore your personal strengths through a quick, free, and confidential quiz. You will receive an instant score and information about how to apply and grow your strengths.

https://bit.ly/3fUy1Od

Chapter Two

# DISCOVERING YOUR TALENT ROOTS

*"We all have our purpose, we all have our strengths."*
*-Beyoncé, American singer and actress (1981- )*

Everyone has talents—qualities or traits we favor. These strengths form the core of our superpowers. If recognized and honed, they are the key for introverts to manage a wide range of situations at home and at work. Your own strengths reside in the eight talents described below. You will lean on several naturally throughout the day, others with brief forethought. Some may not be prolific at all. That is perfectly normal.

Oftentimes in life and in work, people encourage us to fix our weaknesses. We attend training classes to close gaps, but our real focus should be on understanding our strengths. We often have a passion for employing these inherent skills, so practicing and growing them will pay the greatest dividends.

In Beyond Introversion's Introvert Talent Quiz, over 1,350 respondents replied to a myriad of questions to determine which personal traits were strongest for them. Not surprisingly, everybody's responses were different, and yours may vary from these results as well. Yet a few compelling patterns emerged:

1. Common traits: Amongst introverts, the most common traits are planning, observation, thoughtfulness, and learning.

2. Variable traits: Possess traits of loyalty and creativity.

3. Sporadic traits: Resilience and sociability are less common amongst introverts but do occasionally appear.

Although it is likely you favor the more common introvert traits, your strengths may span all three categories, depending on the situation. No one is strong on all eight traits. Focus on growing the top four or five that feel most natural to you. We will reference these traits throughout the book to highlight those that introverts most commonly tap in various situations ranging from meetings and networking to communication and team leadership. These will intertwine with your values and mindsets to form your superpower "trunk."

Remember, your talents may come from any of these groups. Study this list. Take our online Introvert Talent Quiz at https://bit. ly/3fUy10d. Having identified your talents, apply them throughout this book. You can identify the most common traits that support each chapter by the icons noted below.

# COMMON TRAITS

## PLANNING

**Definition: Planning introverts are well organized and thrive on structure and schedules.** You use these skills to detail family vacations and even household tasks. Planners enjoy setting goals that help everyone stay focused and use calendars and task lists to keep on track. You may also enjoy arranging events including home parties or work meetings to maintain a desired level of control over an otherwise chaotic day.

**Grow & Use:** Be sure to have a system. Whether a paper planner or a phone app, such organization will provide you great comfort and alleviate the fear of missing deadlines or obligations. Use your calendar meticulously. Enjoy the freedom of scheduling meetings rather than having to do drop-in chats. Block off private time for deskwork and meeting prep. Offer to arrange dinner parties or work meetings to gain the comfort and familiarity that calms the nerves during these events. Planning may not be glamorous, but it is the foundation for tackling many of the daunting "branches" we will cover in Section II.

**CAUTION:** Planning can become a favorite pastime. That's okay, but don't force the same level of detail on others who don't have a similar need or style.

## OBSERVATION

**Definition: Observant introverts are exceptional listeners.** Introverts use these skills to attend to others, observe scenes, consider both sides of an issue, and think introspectively. Observant introverts may appear to be quiet but are often surveying the landscape and absorbing information. You prefer more time to assess situations and options before declaring a position or view. At home and at work you tend to see situations from a different perspective and take the time to consider other views before moving forward. Remember, listening is learning.

**Grow & Use:** To develop this skill, consciously observe not only words but also body language. Take notes to remember and reinforce meeting details. Repeat what you hear and probe further for more information. This will help to focus your observations and speed up your process to voice opinions.

**CAUTION:** Don't be drawn to make early, verbose pronouncements. Take your time to observe, analyze, consider, and decide. Your views will make a difference.

# THOUGHTFULNESS

**Definition: Thoughtful introverts are predisposed to consider others' opinions and feelings.** Thoughtful people are often highly intuitive, can sense difficult issues, and are respectful of not only other's feelings but also their individual approach and concerns. You take comfort in sharing feelings to bond and genuinely help others.

**Grow & Use:** What a great trait in life—caring for others. You may foster this by nurturing and listening to family and friends. Mindfully consider others' positions on topics and the impact of work decisions. Carve out one-on-one time to build rapport. Most people are not comfortable to develop the personal sharing you crave. The world is filled with verbose and aggressive people. Leaning on your thoughtful nature will balance the room and ensure everyone's positions are taken into consideration.

**CAUTION:** This trait can become burdensome if you overwhelm yourself with other people's issues. Manage your emotions to a moderate level and don't sacrifice your own views just to be empathetic.

# LEARNING

**Definition: Learning introverts are curious.** You love to learn about the world around you. You may be a voracious reader and check out podcasts and YouTube channels, along with TV documentaries. Understanding the history of the world provides context. At home, you may research genealogy or read nonfiction books. At work, gaining background on your company and the projects you are working on helps to bring perspective, may spark creative ideas, and develops loyalty with the group. Make time to quench your thirst for knowledge.

**Grow & Use:** Promote your talent by learning about new subjects. Delve deeper into the background of organizations. Learn another skill at work and understand operations. Consider how processes may become more efficient. Study the culture and history of vacation spots or even the town you live in. Sharing your learning is a great conversation starter as well. Schedule one-on-one sessions with people at work. Calm any shyness by approaching such discussions as learning opportunities. Strive to come away from a conversation with a few points that help build relationships or give you a fresh perspective on a person or team. Start a mentoring relationship or two. Being both a mentor and a mentee will satisfy your desire to learn about yourself and about others.

**CAUTION:** Be aware of the level of information you gather. Don't get overwhelmed by the detail. Don't forget to pick your head up and apply your learning at work and at home.

# VARIABLE TRAITS

## LOYALTY

**Definition: Loyal introverts are strong team players.** They believe in supporting each other, especially when such a bond is reciprocated. In your personal life, you may not have a huge number of friends, but you develop strong bonds with fewer people. You may be a dedicated family person who enjoys dinners around the table together and family games, camping, or vacations. At work, you have a passion for building and maintaining team chemistry. This drives you to build closer relationships and defend your team and company against naysayers.

**Grow & Use:** Build on your talents by developing important relationships. Be wary that not everyone respects loyalty like you do. You may resent it when people are not loyal or respectful of you, so be selective in sharing your loyalties. You are a natural leader. Recognize that hiring people into your work or social "team" is one of your most important tasks. Bad chemistry can destroy your team. While you want a diverse group, confirm they too value trust, loyalty, and teamwork above all. Ensure your team, manager, and other key stakeholders recognize and respect your loyalty.

**CAUTION:** Be careful not to develop "blind" trust. Always be certain your loyalty is well founded so you don't make emotional decisions.

## CREATIVITY

**Definition: Creative introverts rely upon their imagination and resourcefulness to succeed.** At home you are crafty with plenty of hobbies, and you create fun ways to entertain family and friends. Amongst the myriad of deadlines and deliverables, people don't often make the space to be creative at work. However, if you carve out creative daydreaming time, you will bring a unique talent into the workplace that is often admired and rewarded.

**Grow & Use:** Carve out time to develop your talents by exploring hobbies like art or cooking. In business, consider innovative ways of approaching tasks including process redesign. Block off time to imagine on your own. Schedule brainstorming sessions with others. Create a relaxing atmosphere that encourages innovation. Let the ideas flow without the limitations of challenge or editing. Ideas may come fast and furious, so take notes. You may later want to partner with those who can add structure and analysis to your ideas.

**CAUTION:** Seek other's input and be open to the contributions and challenges from those with different perspectives.

# SPORADIC TRAITS

## RESILIENCE

**Definition: Resilient introverts bounce back quickly and have control over their emotions.** You have a full range of emotions—happy, sad, angry, thrilled, frustrated, satisfied—but you choose to use each when appropriate. You will often be applauded for your calmness in difficult situations. Resilient people generally handle surprises and change of plans well. Resilience is a great complement for the planning talent.

**Grow & Use:** Try to remain in the moment, mindful, and present. Don't shy away from using all your emotions at the right time. Calmness in the heat of crisis is an exceptional skill, but an impassioned speech, especially from someone who is typically calm, can be motivating and empowering. Moderation is your friend. Use your desire to be in command to expand your introverted comfort zone and stretch yourself.

**CAUTION:** Don't let your need for control overpower your need to be open-minded toward other peoples' processes. Be thoughtful in your actions.

## SOCIABILITY

**Definition: Social introverts enjoy interaction with others.** This may sound like an extrovert, but all introverts socialize, and many thrive on this interaction in particular circumstances. As an introvert socializer, you likely prefer an environment that you can manage to a degree by selecting the people, venue, and timetable. This reduces the number of uncertain variables and may allow you to gracefully bow out when your energy starts to wane. This is certainly true with strangers but also with friends, co-workers, and even with family.

**Grow & Use:** Hone your conversational talents through practice. Resist your natural inclination to always find and enjoy time alone and reach out for social engagement. You will be glad you did as you are good at socializing and need this community. However, the key to using this strength is to be selective about the people you choose to be with and the duration of the event. Prepare in advance by considering who is going to be there, what topics you want to share, and what questions you may have for the group.

**CAUTION:** Your energy battery will wind down, typically sooner than others. Pay attention to the meter and leave before you are drained. You may wish to announce at the outset that you may have to leave early for a personal obligation.

I think we can all agree that leaders are often under tremendous pressure—and US presidents provide perhaps an extreme example of such hardship. Many presidents face difficult tests thrust upon them, like wars or economic depressions. Others create change through a vision of social reform. Some lead quietly, with reflection, while others steer with higher energy and charisma. Regardless of their style, the best do so authentically. They consider counsel from trusted advisors, they make decisions in line with their values, and they act by utilizing their skills and talents.

Harry Truman was one such president. He followed a formidable four-term president, Franklin D. Roosevelt, and was under immense pressure from internal and external adversaries. Yet Truman acted boldly and decisively to end World War II, shift focus to the looming Cold War, and shape post-war Europe through the Marshall Plan. Truman is considered one of the most introverted presidents in US history.[6] He leaned on his talents of observation, thoughtfulness, and resilience to guide the United States through extraordinarily tenuous times. Today he is recognized as one of the most courageous presidents in our history. He didn't receive many accolades at the time, but as an introvert, I think Truman would have been quite fine with that. Each of us benefits from identifying and practicing our talents so that we can lean upon them for the challenges and opportunities ahead.

## Exploring Your Talents

Your talents are those that come naturally and are most consistent throughout your daily life—when you are relaxing at home with family, when you are under the pressure of deadlines or crises at work, when you are alone, and when you are under the microscope of others. These strengths are also the key to winning the Energy Equation. Using your strengths generates energy for you. Additionally, as you practice and grow your key strengths, you will develop greater confidence to lean on them in the most difficult times.

The chart below indicates the average of each of the eight traits as gathered through the Introvert Talent Quiz. However, keep in mind we are all different. The range of scores varies by over 20% from the average based on our diverse introvert group, so your ordering may be quite different. The ranking of your top three to five talents is more telling than the score itself. Those strengths that are most predominant and comfortable to you are the ones you should focus on expanding.

The horizontal lines designate levels of proficiency: anchor, practice, and explore. Select strengths will be anchor traits—ones that come naturally and which you use frequently. Others you may need to explore further to gain comfort and familiarity. Scores and levels will grow as you explore and practice your key talents.

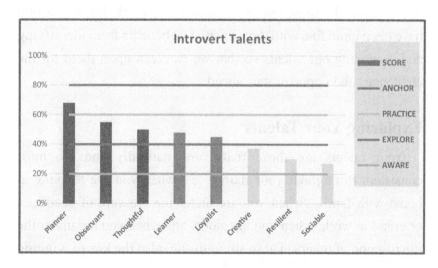

Regina C. of Ohio shares: "I have been criticized all my life for being quiet and independent, and I began to believe that I was weird and unlovable. Now I know that I'm a unique, lovable, kind person; I'm an introvert! And proud of it."

These skills will meld with the rest of your tree's roots to form the strong trunk you need to tackle the traditionally challenging situations at work, which we cover in detail in Section II.

## ACTIONS:

1. Take the Introvert Talent Quiz at https://bit.ly/3fUyl0d. You will receive your personalized results immediately via email.

2. Review the eight traits and consider which are your greatest talents. Write them down and consider how you can practice them at work and at home.

## *The Corporate Introvert* – **Accompanying Worksheets**

Free Worksheets accompany most chapters so you can record your strengths, values, and passions and develop your own plan to apply your talents to become a confident and authentic leader.

https://www.BeyondIntroversion.com/tci-landing-page

# Chapter Three

# STAY TRUE TO
# YOUR VALUE ROOTS

*"Who you are, what your values are, what you stand for,*
*they are your anchor, your north star.*
*You'll find them in your soul."*
—*Anne Mulcahy, first female CEO and later chairperson of Xerox*
*(1952- )*

Our inherent talents alone will not guide us through the maze of difficult workplace situations. We need another critical type of root that feeds our trees: values. Values provide you with direction during chaotic times or complex choices. Unlike your strengths, there are no particular "introvert values." However, given the reflective nature of introverts, we are more apt to discover and lean on our values throughout life. Successful, happy, and confident people often know their core values and how to apply them.[7]

## Self-Validation

What are values? Why are they important? What are your values?

Values are your core beliefs. They are principles that drive you. They are handrails that provide support on your personal journey. They aren't specific activities. They are more like tenets that are so much a part of you that they drive your decisions, often subconsciously. They help you set priorities. They give you a warm, satisfying feeling when followed but a nagging feeling in the back of your mind when they are violated.

Values don't tend to fluctuate much. Yes, they may change over time as your life changes. You may, for example, have more ambitious values as you enter the workforce, and you may have more philanthropic values as you gain a level of security and wealth. However, values don't generally change in the short term, and certainly not daily or based on specific circumstances. If they seem to, they are not really your guiding values.

Esteemed leadership guru and author John Maxwell recognizes: "If I have strong values on the inside, I need less validation from the outside."[8] Understanding and leaning on our values provides just the confidence boost and conviction that we need.

## Discovering Your Values

Many people have already dedicated time to discover their values. Others can't list even a few of their tenets, as they reside in their subconscious. Some may present them in a generic sort of way – trust, honesty, or being a good person. While these might be true, discovering your values may require deeper introspection. We are all different and our values reflect our unique upbringings, spiritual beliefs, and life experiences. For those who may be challenged to recall their bedrock values, find a quiet, private place to work through this four-step Values Discovery Process[9]:

### Values Discovery Process

1. **Consider important life moments.** Jot down poignant memories with your family or friends, at work, or at your place of worship. Those recollections are often moments ripe with lessons. MindTools.com suggests asking yourself three questions:

   • What moments were you the happiest or the saddest?

   • What moments were you most proud or most embarrassed?

   • What moments were you most satisfied or frustrated?

   These may take time to remember. Consider your work assignments, your special times growing up, and family memories. Contemplate what you were doing in these circumstances. Why were you proud or fulfilled? Write down a few situations for each of these questions. Set this list aside.

2. **Brainstorm your values.** There are many online pick lists for values, but these principles and beliefs really need to come from you. You need to do the work of considering what has driven key choices in your life. What is most important to you? This shouldn't be too difficult or take long. Jot down any values that come to mind. Once you get rolling, this list may grow to twenty or thirty. When your ideas run dry, step back for a while. You may then consult an online resource to supplement.

3. **Return to the poignant moments you listed in step 1.** Which of your values in step 2 relate to any of those moments? This will help you narrow down your list. You will find values that are quite similar and can fit together. Others may be too narrow, fitting only one situation, while some are too broad. You will relate to several quickly and others just may not feel right. Don't worry about word choice or grammar. Use the word(s) that mean something to you. Let your intuition guide you in selecting around five core beliefs.

4. **Prioritize your list.** This may be difficult to do as different situations call upon different values, but there will be times when your principles may be in conflict. Which ones are truly unshakeable?

   As you seek to narrow your list, reflect on whether each item feels like you.

   **These are your values.**

## Three Considerations

In recalling your values or documenting them through the Values Discovery Process, consider these three conditions:

First, your values may often overlap and support each other. For instance, a sense of **responsibility** and **initiative** may be driven by your need to provide **security** for your family.

Second, certain values may keep other values in check. A value to **achieve**, for instance, is virtuous, unless you sacrifice **honesty**, morals, and innocent bystanders in order to satisfy this value at all costs. Hence, mindfulness keeps you on an honorable path.

Third, you may notice that your strengths and values match up. When your talents complement your values and your principles support your strengths, your roots are stronger and will fortify your tree to thrive.

## Applying Your Values

Remember your values. Write them down and put them on your desk. Practicing your values may come naturally, but the true test is when you are faced with complex, difficult decisions. Many of those situations are complicated by emotions, expectations, or outside influence from managers, co-workers, or counterparties, which can make decision-making grueling. Exert patience when key decisions arise and make sure you lead with values rather than emotions. Stepping back and reviewing how your values fit with your options will often reveal the best decision.

Your principles are not what others believe or what you think "should" drive you. Values will consistently steer you to make decisions—whether you are in a meeting of ten, a room of 100, or all by yourself with no one looking.

## Sharing Values is Powerful Leadership

Values often arise from personal stories, an example of right or wrong that has stuck with you over the years. Thus, we often hesitate to share such an intimate topic. However, exchanging values can be enormously powerful. Individuals leap to a higher level of trust and teams can identify how they complement each other in pursuit of the group's goals. You can share your values either in a private chat with a close co-worker, or in a team workshop constructed as a respectful, non-judgmental teambuilding exercise.

During such sessions, you will certainly have different values and may not agree with other's beliefs, but that is the diversity which strong, productive teams aim to achieve. Rather than challenging others' values, simply be curious about them and the stories behind them. Create the space for everyone to share if they wish. What are your values? How did you determine that? How have they helped you make decisions?

Once everyone has shared, pose the question of how this discussion may help each of the team members and group overall. Should the team adjust assignments to leverage someone's values? Did people gain insights on how to communicate better? Perhaps the biggest benefit is in team bonding. Such a result may sound nebulous, but team trust and chemistry are invaluable and critical components of organizational success.

## Don't Fake It 'Til You Make It

Many in the work world are induced or even coached to "fake it 'til you make it." This advice may be intended to cover technical topics that you are still learning. We are all new at a role for a while—on average, about a dozen times during our career.

However, all too often this phrase applies to an introvert's overall approach. This may lead us to put on a façade rather than let others see our true self. Sharon Pastor, Lead Procurement Manager, notes: " I can relate to the mask as I have worn one for 19 years. I am constantly told by male managers to act differently and even have been bullied and discriminated against on numerous occasions, causing risk normalization on my part." Have you been concerned others may question your expertise, your social skills, or your self-confidence? These fears often lead us to put on a mask that only comes off when we are commuting home. The mask fits so well in the office that we may feel like we match the cultural norms around us.

At times it may appear easier to try to be someone we are not and to block people from knowing the real you. The life of the gregarious and confident co-worker seems so much easier and simpler than ours. However, theirs is not the life for us. Trying to make it so only leaves us confused and belittled.

I adopted this "fake it 'til you make it" approach for most of my career. I pushed myself to be as social and spontaneous as others. I just wanted to fit in. As a result, I led two separate lives—one at work and one at home. And truth be told, my family didn't see the real me, either, as I was so exhausted from the strain of acting all day that I was lazy and withdrawn at home. As the pressure mounted with my career trajectory rising, I found I needed alcohol and excessive eating to best cope. The damage to my health, self-confidence, and family life were almost irreversible.

I always assumed others at work saw through my façade, but I didn't dare ask. Nor could I reveal my true self. When I retired after thirty years, I shared my plans to write my memoir about my introverted life to a room full of colleagues spanning the totality of my career. Nearly everyone was shocked to hear my plans and especially the declaration of my own introversion. "You aren't an introvert!" so many exclaimed. I smirked that I had pulled off such a grand caper, yet I recalled the damage I had inflicted upon myself and recognized the lost opportunities I had missed with others.

I had cheated myself of comfort and confidence, and I had cheated my work team of knowing my true self and gaining my unique perspectives. Our highest calling is to be authentic—to be ourselves. This helps us to be happy and aligned, and it brings a unique perspective and voice into the room. As painful as it may appear at first, others need and want to get your true opinion. That diversity of perspective is exactly what makes teams so valuable and companies successful.

So rather than "fake it," I implore you to learn from my experiences and those of many others. You don't need to change; you just need to embrace your true values and talents, allowing your authentic self to shine.

Understanding your values and strengths and being honest with yourself will gain you tremendous respect from others, and more importantly a sense of serene confidence for yourself.

## A Gift to Yourself

Values give us the confidence and courage to make the right choices without being swayed by what others might do. This may be especially tough in the work setting if your values conflict with those of your employer, boss, or customer. You feel that you must compromise your values to align with others or else risk your job, reputation, or security. These are real-life choices that may require discussion with your manager, human resources, legal, or compliance officer within your organization. Only you can gauge your comfort in violating your values to preserve your job. If you find these situations unbearable, this is not the right job for you. You should consider a change of role or company. The nagging guilt of violating your values can be overwhelming. It is your conscience telling you something is not right. This is not the time to question your values but to question your situation or the action others are requesting of you.

Be aware of your values and adhere to them through the choices you make. The reflective nature of introverts often lends itself to greater awareness of values that provide the bedrock for your decisions. However, that same introspection can weigh heavily if you violate these principles. Let your values be your guide.

## ACTIONS:

1.  Recall your values or use the Values Discovery Process to explore and document your values.

2.  Pause in the midst of complex, emotional circumstances to make choices aligned with your values.

3.  Seek an opportunity to exchange values with a co-worker or with your team.

Chapter Four

# MINDSET NOURISHES YOUR ROOTS

*"Always bear in mind that your own resolution to succeed is more important than any other thing."*
*−Abraham Lincoln, 16th US President during the Civil War and Emancipation (1809-1865)*

Confidence is often considered a key catalyst for successful people; one which many introverts lack in the early phases of their journey and scramble to build later in life. If talents and values are the roots that support our tree, positive mindset is like the water so vital to nourishing our roots. It provides the energy our core needs to become strong and grow. Without enough cultivation, our talents will flounder. We will lack the confidence to successfully tackle the work challenges that frustrate so many introverts.

Too often introverts suffer from cluttered minds and self-inflicted wounds. An introspective nature is prone to regret and rerun of the past or fear and worry about the future. While past experiences provide fresh learning ground and great memories and the future is filled with dreams and excitement, our focus belongs on the present. If we bring our attention to the present and cultivate a positive attitude, our talents and values will grow, and our confidence will bloom.

I offer five mindsets that can release our strengths to work for us: 1) employing moderation, 2) focusing on what we can control, 3) practicing self-compassion, 4) championing vulnerability, and 5) chasing passions. Two people may be faced with the same issues at work, but one approaches the challenge with vigor and energy while the other appears unmotivated, distracted, or weighed down with negativity. The difference in results can be staggering.

In our Introvert Leadership Quiz, over 90% of respondents said they are aware of these positive mindset skills, yet only 40% employ them frequently. Use this chapter as an opportunity to reflect on your mindset at work and to gather tips to build your confidence further.

The great news is that we can shift our mindset. With a proper frame of mind, our strengths can approach their full potential and we will be well on our way toward creating the success and satisfaction we desire.

## #1 Employ Moderation

*"Everything must be structured around the center. The excessive stretching of the consciousness of responsibility... already has been broken asunder in the world ...*
*For the most serious human evil is lack of moderation."*
*–Helmuth Plessner*

Have you ever climbed Mount Kilimanjaro or completed a marathon? Adrenalin-pumping adventure can be the spice of life. Flourishing introverts do not lack the ambition or initiative to achieve, but they need self-control to moderate their fervor to remain both balanced and sustainable. Life in general and in the corporate world in particular is better suited for moderation. It may be more exciting to run a marathon than jog a few miles on a treadmill, but running marathons routinely, working 60-hour weeks, or socializing weeknights and weekends invites injury, burnout, excessive eating or drinking, or other repercussions that make those lifestyle choices unsustainable.

Moderation may not offer the glitz and glamour of the extreme, but it provides agility, stability, and sustainability.

- **Agility** equips us to roll with the punches when troubles arise, rather than be so glued to an approach that we freeze. Change is inevitable, so remaining flexible is essential.

- **Stability** in our lives is crucial for contentment and flourishing. You need to balance what's important to you, which may encompass physical and mental health, family, spirituality, work ambitions, or hobbies. When we intensely pursue one aspect of our lives, we often sacrifice others and jeopardize our overall balance and wellbeing.

- Finally, moderation provides a feasible and **sustainable** path to maintain and enjoy those items that are important in your life.

Finding moderation or balance in our lives is tricky, but essential for a productive and fulfilling lifestyle. A mindset of moderation alleviates the pressure to chase the extreme because you place greater value on the balance. To find that balance, jot down your most important life goals. Review them periodically and be mindful of them when you are making decisions. Shifting our mindset to celebrate moderation helps build confidence and contentment.

## #2 Focus on What You Control

*"Grant me the serenity to accept the things I cannot change; the courage to change the things I can; and the wisdom to know the difference."*
*—Serenity Prayer*

The Serenity Prayer offers powerful words as we set our mind toward the challenges ahead. Life presents us with many opportunities, yet often we waste our time and energy focusing on things outside our control.

For example, as an author I would like to reach a large audience with my message and place my books in the hands of introverts around the world. These may be my goals, but I can't sign others up to my website or force people to buy my book. These items are out of my control. Worrying about them is futile. However, I may be able to influence these goals by writing a quality book, creating an interesting website, and using social media and blogs to reach out to my audience. These are in my control. I should be focusing my time on those actions.

Unfortunately, many people expend energy on objectives or conditions out of their control. We can get drawn into ultra-competitive environments and swept up to chase targets that we have no genuine interest in. Yet we have the power to determine our goals and resist distractions along the way.

As introverts striving to manage our Energy Equation, squandering our energy leaves us depleted and distracted from those items we can and should be focused on. If you feel overwhelmed, spend a few minutes listing those items occupying your mind, your calendar, and your action list under either the "I Control" or "Others Control" column. This will help you reallocate your time and energy and will change your goals to be more inwardly focused on what you can affect.

## #3 Practice Self-Compassion

*"Remember, you have been criticizing yourself for years and it hasn't worked. Try approving of yourself and see what happens."*
*–Louise Hay*

It's no surprise that many introverts can be their own worst critics. We denigrate ourselves – at work *(I should have done better. This is not my best work. I should have spoken up in that meeting.)* and at home *(I could do more around the house. Why didn't I talk more? Why can't I get in shape?)*. If we wrote down words or lines that we say or think to ourselves throughout the day, it would sound like a horror story written by an abusive adversary. We hope to counterbalance all of that negative self-talk with scant pieces of positive reinforcement from others–like our families or managers.

Instead, we should aim for self-compassion. As Kristin Neff, author of *Self-Compassion: The Proven Power of Being Kind to Yourself,* states: "people who are compassionate toward their failings and imperfections experience greater well-being than those who repeatedly judge themselves."[10] Try looking inward. It's time to spend a lot less energy pining over what others think and more effort encouraging ourselves to succeed and celebrating our journey along the way.

Let's support ourselves through Positive Self Talk (PST). Try saying supportive words of encouragement and recognition rather than beating yourself up. Some examples:

*I am well prepared and will do great on my presentation.*

*The Corporate Introvert*

*I will lead an engaging, interactive, and productive meeting.*
*I did an awesome job on the research for that project.*

Before events, close your eyes and envision a successful meeting, networking session, or project presentation. Then share words of encouragement out loud or write them down. It's amazing how these simple actions change our mindset. It's like getting that pat on the back throughout the day.

During the day, make sure you recognize your accomplishments before you consider things you could do better. Capture and celebrate your list of achievements in a journal. Include the big project triumphs but also the personal victories such as attending socials, leading meetings, or learning unique skills. Scour this list later to substantiate your successes at your annual management review or scan it when you need a boost.

Rather than being your own worst critic, it's time to be your greatest fan!

## #4 Champion Vulnerability

*"Vulnerability sounds like truth and feels like courage. Truth and courage aren't always comfortable, but they are never weakness."*
*-Brené Brown*

Adopting a mindset of vulnerability is difficult because it requires that we step outside of our comfort zone and try something different. Vulnerability invites risk–the risk of being exposed and the risk of failure. If we share personal stories at work that expose our own introversion, others may sense insecurities or pain associated with our sharing in such an open way. What if they don't understand or, worse yet, what if they mock us?

However, such vulnerability has the power to change relationships, team culture, and self-confidence. You will strike a strong bond with those who do appreciate the openness. It's a great opportunity to practice making an impact with others as we become role models for authenticity, strength and bravery.

We also accept risk when we put ourselves out there in various work situations, challenging others' perspectives and offering our own opinions. These are important work exchanges when done in a tactful way. It requires courage to do so and, yes, occasionally we invite arguments and disputes, but we can be proud to have exercised our values and made our thoughts known.

People often assume that introverts lack boldness and conviction. However, embracing your strengths and authenticity will help you to extend yourself. The key is to bring your voice into the room when you have passion about a topic, key knowledge to share, or conviction in your heart that gives you the courage to rise up. The more you practice being vulnerable, the more you will learn about yourself and transform your self-image to one of bravery and pride.

## #5 Chase Your Passion

*"Passion is energy. Feel the power that comes from focusing*
*on what excites you."*
*—Oprah Winfrey*

Recall from your childhood or perhaps parenting moments as an adult. We expose children to many different experiences. Otherwise, they will never know if they like gymnastics, art, or robotics. So we sign them up for various classes. Some of them they hate, others are okay, and once in a while they land on a hobby or skill that overjoys them and perhaps changes their life. My son tried soccer but was more enamored with the leaves and grass that scattered the pitch than the sport itself. He tried basketball but never found joy in the game. Then he discovered singing and piano, and it became the backbone of his life. He sings and plays constantly, he looks forward to practicing and learning, and he's grown confident on the stage. Music often serves as his introduction to new friends and bonding with like-minded people. He discovered a lifelong passion.

Yet as adults, people often dismiss the word passion. It's too fanciful for many. When someone states that they should follow their passion in life and in their career, often people chuckle and insist that life doesn't work that way. It is "work," after all.

Understand your passion and search for opportunities to cultivate that passion. What are your passions? They are things you thoroughly enjoy. They are not limited to your hobbies or family activities. It's not only acceptable but should be expected that you have some passions at work. Your eyes may twinkle and your face may light up when you talk about them well after work is over. You are not at a loss for words when you share a project or cause that you believe in. You often lose track of time while enjoying your interests. What do you truly love to do? What stands out in your day? Perhaps it's project management or building relationships or helping others. You may gravitate to a task such as developing a cohesive team or a value such as delivering on time or providing exceptional customer service.

If you are doing an activity you enjoy, it acts as a catalyst to build your talent roots. Then, even the uncomfortable social engagements, spontaneous hallway debates, and abrupt challenges by your management will seem a lot easier as part of your journey to live your purpose and pursue your dreams. Don't consider your passions as unworthy. Such a pursuit is noble and will make all the difference in your life.

I urge you to identify your passions and strive to make them part of your journey. Even if you can't find a dream job, at least work in a job that is exciting, challenging, and fulfilling for you. If that is so, you will have many more good days than bad. You will be purpose-driven, looking forward to most every day. Chase that aspiration.

Often introverts gaze at loud and overbearing people with a sense of envy until we eventually recognize our path is different yet equally satisfying. When we embrace the concepts of employing moderation, focusing on what we can control, practicing self-compassion, championing vulnerability, and chasing our passions, we become stronger with the right mix of confidence, humility, and drive to stand tall and be proud. Take steps to practice these positive approaches. Your tree cannot survive without water. Nourish your roots frequently and you will defeat your limitations and free yourself to flourish.

## ACTIONS:

1. Review the cautions for each strength, as noted in Chapter 2. Employing these will encourage moderation when applying your talents.

2. Consider the five mindsets (moderation, control, self-compassion, vulnerability, and passions):

   a. Which are well incorporated into your current approach?

   b. Which would you like to focus on for improvement?

c. Jot down a couple of actions you plan to take to break a habit and change your mindset.

3. Record both personal and work goals to help maintain life's balance.

4. Complete an "In My Control/Out of My Control" list when you feel overwhelmed.

5. Incorporate Positive Self Talk and journaling to support your self-compassion.

6. Make note of your "awesome" days. Then explore the passions that ignited that excitement.

Chapter Five

# AMBITION FEEDS GROWTH

*"Everyone can rise above their circumstances and achieve success
if they are dedicated to and passionate about what they do."*
*−Nelson Mandela, South African revolutionary and political
leader (1918-2013)*

Our strengths and values are our core traits. Our mindset determines how well we apply those traits. However, many brilliant, charismatic, optimistic people never achieve anywhere close to their potential. Meanwhile, many people with average intellect go on to achieve great things. Our future is not determined by smart vs. brilliant or interesting vs. magnetic. The catalyst for our future is the level of our drive and ambition and willingness to grow along the way. These key factors are essential in launching people toward their personal dreams and leadership success.

This is especially true for introverts. Introverts may be considered underdogs in many ways. We don't meet the societal norms. We don't have the loudest voice in the room, so we are often discounted and have a taller mountain to climb to be noticed, heard, and recognized for the great contributions we make. Even well-informed extroverts acknowledge introverts face greater challenges at home and at work. Yet we have our own unique strengths that enable us to contribute and lead as much as anyone else. To extend our tree analogy, ambition is our innate drive to achieve—the nutrients naturally imbedded in the soil around our roots. Growth comes from the drive we attain by stretching our comfort zone, our added fertilizer if you will. Ambition and growth together provide the initiative and determination to help us climb up that steeper mountain.

## Ambition

Ambition is our inner drive to grow, learn, and succeed. Too many people are satisfied with where they are or what they have. This may be complacency or fear–fear of the unknown, of change, or of extending our comfort zone.

Yet introverts are especially filled with ambition. We want to succeed–to provide for our families, to be recognized by others, to take pride in our accomplishments–like others. However, our path is often more challenging than most. We must draw beyond our natural inclinations to succeed.

For introverts with a defined comfort zone, our favorite day may be one spent at home, with a book and a journal and occasionally a close friend or two. That scene brings warmth and relaxation. No tension, no expectations, no other standards to live up to. But we all know there is more to a fulfilling life than remaining in our cocoon.

While I'm sure extroverts would say they, too, are stretching, I think it is different. When introverts stretch, we push against our biggest fears and a society that often belittles our approach.

Extroverts, on the other hand, are already outgoing and spontaneous. They may find it uncomfortable to be more reflective and spend time alone, but few extroverts will be forced into those moments or be required to do so by managers or society as a whole. So, kudos to introverts for getting out there.

We want to succeed, to satisfy our curiosity to learn, to be proud of ourselves, and to reach toward our purpose and passions that ripen in our heads during our reflective moments. This is our ambition. However, leaping far outside our comfort zone can be frightening and overwhelming. We need guidance on how to apply these ambitions through a series of modest stretches, without activating the panic that can accompany extending beyond our comfort zone.

## The Growth Rings Model

The Growth Rings Model (GRM) acts as our fertilizer—a powerful and systematic way to enhance our innate abilities to pursue our ambitions. The Model provides a simple approach for gaining experience and building confidence. Pairing the Growth Rings Model with positive mindsets of control and self-compassion, you will be prepared to take incremental yet bold steps to change your own approach. I'll provide the basics and then offer an example to illuminate the process.

We start at the center, our core.

- Our natural comfort zone is **Home Base**. We feel most at ease here. We could stay here all day doing what we enjoy most.
- Our **Neighborhood** is just beyond our home. Here, we are not straying far away. We use our strengths and values but in different ways. This is often comforting and rewarding.

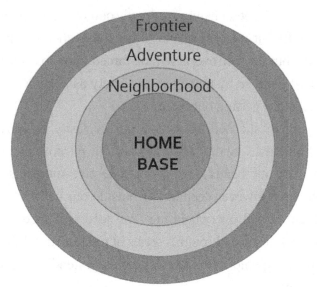

- In the **Adventure** ring, we are trekking further away. We are using our strengths, but we are pushing ourselves into unfamiliar environments or situations. This would be quite a leap from our Home Base but extending first to our Neighborhood makes this next step more manageable. We still may be anxious about this step, but often curious enough to try, as the incentives—whether they be pride, happiness, or financial—tempt us.

- The **Frontier** ring is a monumental challenge. We are far from home, completely out of our original comfort zone. We may try this escapade to challenge ourselves, because the motivation is significant, our confidence has been strengthened from our journey thus far, or because our ambitions drive us further. This stage brings a lot of apprehension, and we may decline the opportunity altogether. On the other hand, we may be forced to this ring by an unexpected job loss, a major life transition, or a new work project.

Though simple, the Growth Rings Model can be quite powerful, and applies to work situations, relationships, exercise, and more. Select an area you have been pondering for a while and employ the model. Free worksheets are available at www.BeyondIntroversion. com/tci-landing-page.

Let's use a marketing example to help bring the model to life:

When I rekindled my writing ambitions as retirement approached, I just wanted to write. I paid no attention to the publishing or marketing tasks that would follow. It's a good thing I didn't, because marketing felt foreign to me and might have scared me away from writing altogether. There's a nugget of learning I stumbled upon here – set ambitious goals but focus on the next incremental step to avoid untimely anxiety. Nonetheless, once my book was complete, I was faced with the prospect of marketing— of engaging others with my story in order to build followers and share my message.

Using the Growth Rings Model, even my **Home Base** felt a little daunting. However, I love to write, so posting my first book on Amazon with a description was new but manageable. I could have stopped there, but after spending two years writing my memoir, *In Search of Courage: An Introvert's Story*, I wanted to get my message out there. I was proud of my story and hoped others could benefit from my journey.

I expanded into my **Neighborhood** ring by blogging on my website and writing guest articles for other publications. This used my writing skills and passion in a different way. Though it was a stretch for me, I became comfortable and proud of my accomplishments. I began to consider further growth.

In-person or virtual engagement with strangers both belong in my **Adventure** ring. I'm much less comfortable, and butterflies form in my stomach just contemplating this step. Though I can plan for these discussions, there is an element of thinking on the fly and not controlling the dialogue that always makes me fearful. However, I took the leap and scheduled a podcast interview. I was determined to try rather than forever regret the unknown. I planned my discussion, practiced answers to anticipated questions, assumed the right mindset, and reframed my nervousness into excitement by envisioning a successful podcast. I coached myself through positive self talk in the days leading up to the event.

Although I still get nervous, after dozens of podcasts I've grown to truly enjoy the interaction. It's a chance for me to share my passion. I know the topic, after all, and I frame it as a one-on-one talk since I can't see the dozens or hundreds of attendees listening in. I was so proud of pushing myself to achieve something that scared me to death when I gazed beyond the Neighborhood Ring.

I've glanced out at my **Frontier** ring—presentations in front of larger crowds—and have recently begun to frame an Introvert's Mentoring Circle program. This will surely challenge me further, but I'm excited to create a platform that uses my leadership and coaching strengths to grow personally and meet my outreach objectives.

The Growth Rings Model can also apply to an exercise program, such as running, or business aspects like networking and leadership, which we will examine later. You need look no further than new challenges you are eyeing with nervous trepidation to find applications for the Growth Rings Model.

# The Regret Theory

It's relatively easy to stay at Home Base or to limit your outings to the Neighborhood ring. However, progressing to your Adventure or Frontier rings can be angst-ridden. If you are tempted to stop your journey, consider the Regret Theory. Will you regret never trying that next ring? If you decide you truly won't, it may not be that important. On the other hand, if you believe you will regret not at least attempting to stretch further, than keep driving to that next ring. Our moderation mindset suggests applying your energy to small, incremental steps for those growth projects that are most important to you.

## Stretch Kindly

Be bold and courageous in applying the Growth Rings Model to your greatest fears and dreams. Balance this with a commitment to "stretch kindly," applying your mindset principles around moderation and self-compassion in your journey. Marcia Cottros shares that: "in the last five years I have tried to live by the idea that life is a journey and not a destination. In focusing on the journey, I have found that getting to the destination is more enjoyable, less stressful, and the destination is usually overall better."

Yes, follow your ambitions to extend your comfort zone. Be adventurous. Aim higher. However, always do this with joy and self-compassion. Give yourself permission to stop or try a different path. Rebecca Weiner, educational consultant and creator of Learn Play Grow offers this: "I struggle with gearing up to go out of my comfort zone and then retreating and repeating. What I learned is the idea that retreating is self-compassion, not cowardice. It's balance back and forth, not constant forward motion." Indeed, the victory is not in crawling across the finish line, exhausted and regretting the journey itself, but exploring paths to learn and grow. True satisfaction is not in where you are on the rings, but in the journey itself——of taking the chance to stretch kindly.

## Keys to Traveling the Rings

Now that the concepts and applicability are clear, here are tips for how to travel from Home Base toward the outer rings:

- Envision what achieving the next ring will look like. Picture the growth, expertise, and pride that you will feel.
- Plan and prepare which task you want to work on with practical steps to move outward.
- Implement tiny steps, rather than giant leaps to scary places.
- Seek support and advice in your journey from others who have been there.
- Step back and retry if you don't first succeed but still have the hunger to pursue.
- Stretch kindly by gauging your excitement and your apprehension.
- It is not always about reaching the Frontier ring. Celebrate your efforts and your accomplishments wherever you land.

When you couple your innate ambitions with the Growth Rings Model, your roots and tree become stronger. The greatest bonus you will receive is self-confidence. Gill Hasson, author of *Mindfulness,*[11] wisely suggests: "Confidence is not about what you can or can't do, it's what you think or believe you can or can't do." When you stretch your comfort zone, you will find a whole new world. More importantly, you will discover how much more you can do. Even small, incremental trips across the Growth Rings are accomplishments that will swell your pride and grow your confidence to tackle the most daunting work tasks, so you can be the leader you aspire to be.

Your roots, nourished with the water and minerals they need, have now become your superpowers. Together, your talents, values, mindsets, and ambitions provide strong branches which you will next learn how to flex in order to tackle imposing obstacles at work.

## ACTIONS:

1. Consider your ambitions and dreams. What are they? Jot them down to help extend your comfort zone in new directions.

2. Select one challenging task or hobby in your life that you wish to grow. Employ the Growth Rings Model to stretch your comfort zone. Be patient and self-compassionate. Celebrate your journey and successes along the way.

## SECTION II:

# FLEXING YOUR BRANCHES

In Section I you connected with your roots——your strengths, values, and mindsets. We dispelled stereotypes and myths and we discovered how we can build confidence by embracing introversion to do things our way.

Now, with a strong foundation of superpowers, you can apply your strengths, values, and mindsets to grow expansive branches. Each of an introvert's most common branches or work frustrations —uncertainty or change, communications, meetings, and networking—can be converted from obstacles to assets by leaning on the strengths of your roots and applying tailored approaches.

This section builds on your superpowers to remove the fear of work situations that you may think of as challenging for introverts. Let's debunk those myths and provide you with the tools to succeed.

Dr. Ty Belknap tries to console others by stating: "Change happens when the pain of staying where you are becomes greater than the pain of moving." But is it really that troublesome?

Sara F. confesses: "I do a poor job of communicating… to my manager and others. I have this ingrained sense it shouldn't be necessary, but it is."

Steven M. admits: "It seems intimidating to speak out in meetings sometime."

And Drew F. surmises: "When I actually need to network or get a lead, I freeze up and suddenly forget how to even form a cohesive thought."

Many introverts have been conditioned to see these situations as overwhelming. Indeed, they can be if we attempt to manage them as extroverts do. On the surface, these challenges appear to require personal engagement, quick thinking, or self-advocacy. In Section II we will learn how to employ your strengths to conquer each of these situations so you can confidently get your voice in the room and grow your awesome branches.

Chapter Six

# EMERGING AS A
# CHANGE LEADER

*"Change will not come if we wait for some other person or some other time. We are the ones we've been waiting for.*
*We are the change that we seek."*
*–Barack Obama, 44th President of the United States (1961- )*

## Change is Everywhere

Change is all around us. Sometimes we need to react, and other times we can be the catalyst for change. Many introverts would not consider either path as their forte, yet by focusing on our strengths, we can become change leaders.

US presidents offer a perfect example of the different types of change many people experience. For instance, Franklin Roosevelt, Woodrow Wilson, and Harry Truman led the US through changes thrust upon the country like the Great Depression, World War I, and ideological movements such as Communism. Others sought to initiate change to improve American freedoms, lifestyle, and prosperity such as Abraham Lincoln, Lyndon Johnson, and Theodore Roosevelt. Still others—like Herbert Hoover leading up to the 1929 Crash, James Buchanan at the apex of the slavery divide, and Richard Nixon at the height of the Vietnam War—appeared to freeze, unable to muster the courage to either react with integrity or create positive transformation.

While your mission may not appear so grand, you too have the chance to be a change leader—or to be someone who watches as opportunities pass you by. This chapter offers four approaches to change so you may assess your natural inclinations. Then we will cover three components to becoming a change leader.

## Types of Change Agents

Let's consider four extremely different approaches to change. At times, we may fall into any one of these categories based on the situation, sense of urgency, or our emotional state. Understanding your natural inclinations will enable you to reflect and become the change leader every team needs.

1. **Change Resistant**: These are people who thoroughly dislike change. We may all be creatures of habit but change resistors may feel their whole world and all their plans are falling apart. They don't challenge impending change with thoughtful considerations. They fight change and may undermine necessary transformation, even from those in authority. Emotions often fuel this resistance. Change resistors may feel personally threatened by the change and spiteful toward the originator. In either case, there is no good role for change resistors in the

workplace. If you feel this describes you, I suggest evaluating the Shifting Your Mindset section below.

2. **Change Tolerant**: People in this group aren't big fans of change either, although they often tolerate change because it comes from a position of authority. Thus, they don't undermine change, but they rarely initiate alternatives because it doesn't appear to be in their wheelhouse or seems too risky. Team members and leaders eventually identify the tolerators and become frustrated with their lack of positive contributions. If this sounds familiar, focus on the section on Finding Change below.

3. **Change Enthusiast**: Being an enthusiast sounds positive, but often comes from an emotional origin. Many people are enamored by the idea of change. They love to change focus, team structure, approaches—nearly anything is fair game. Some are idea people—they generate and/or pick up on new concepts with zeal. However, change enthusiasts often implement those ideas without thoughtful consideration or discussion. They may advocate and initiate changes because it gives them power over people and activities. Enthusiasts may not realize that flippant change confuses others, dampens the value of prudent change, and eventually erodes the power they are seeking to create. Change enthusiasts should focus on the section about Implementing Good Change below.

4. **Change Leader**: Change leaders use their strengths and positive mindset to seek, create, and support valued change. They evaluate ideas, solicit input from stakeholders, and exert patience before implementing changes. Change leaders consider how to calm the enthusiasts while bringing the tolerators on board. They build credibility through a thoughtful and purposeful process.

Sometimes you will need to adapt to outside changes, just as FDR and Truman did, while other times you should be advocating changes, like Lincoln and LBJ. In either case, the change leader will exercise the best approach for positive, applicable change.

Which type of change agent are you?

## How to Become a Change Leader

Regardless of which type of change agent you profess to be today, you can become a strong change leader by practicing these three approaches:

## Shifting Your Mindset

First recognize that change is everywhere. Without change, the world wouldn't have the technologies and products we enjoy today. Society would not have evolved to recognize the diversity and inclusion that has broadened our world and our workplace. And our businesses would not be able to efficiently produce materials economically. Change is necessary.

However, especially given an introvert's propensity to plan, changes can become overwhelming. That calendar you had set up for the next week collapses when you are called out of town. The topic of that meeting you had prepared for suddenly is altered. Your networking buddy can't join you at the industry cocktail. The manager you worked tirelessly to build rapport and alignment with gets transferred and a new manager arrives. All of these can require tweaks to your plan or even dramatic changes. These situations can be awfully frustrating, and emotions can take over. You may be upset that all the time you spent planning has gone awry. And what's more, you are no longer prepared for the meeting, the networking event, or the new manager. This is a natural reaction and is a hazard of the excessive planning so many introverts revel in.

If change makes you angry, consider the emotions driving this frustration. Perhaps it's concern as your well-prepared plans get scrapped or maybe jealousy for those people grandstanding new ideas? These are understandable feelings for keen planners and those more composed introverts. Harness self-compassion as you seek to broaden your perspective. Console yourself that your plans can be flexible, and you will rework them later. Understand you are at a pivotal moment. You can either become a cancer on the team or a valuable contributor. Lean on your strengths to approach this change as a learning moment and creative opportunity.

Although you may not have total control over the change, if you engage with others to discuss the ideas, challenge select aspects and enhance others in order to make it a more palatable change, you become a positive force instead of a detractor.

## Finding Change

Many companies don't make time for brainstorming and many introverts don't consider it a natural strength. The key is to carve out space to tap your skills. You are busy all day with planning, meetings, discussions, and finally returning home with your own set of inevitable challenges and priorities to manage. These tasks often engage the more structured left side of the brain. Inspiration for change comes from your creative right side. You can foster this brainstorming by carving out time within the right environment.

You may find that favorite activities like reading, journaling, walking, and meditating put you in the brainstorming zone. During each activity you might find your mind drifting away from daily tasks. This is natural and inviting. Let yourself go. Your mind will begin to think of bottlenecks and issues and often creative solutions. Stay in the zone. Don't inhibit your ideas by challenging the rationale or feasibility at this stage. Just as sleep dreams often pass, these daydreams will vanish, so be sure to take notes or leave yourself a voicemail message to capture just a few points so you can expound on them later.

Sara Bonario, Director of Renewable Fuels at a mid-sized energy company, shares: "My special time has always been when I was jogging or walking my dog. There is value in letting your mind wander and rest without expectations. New ideas may not come, but by settling your mind you are better prepared to cope with the changes or challenges you are facing."

Other venues for such brainstorming may include training classes and conferences. While these are not usually calming activities for introverts, these events extract you from daily tasks and open space for daydreaming. You may find you return to work with a few specific tips on the training or conference subject matter, but pages of other brainstorming ideas to consider.

By nature, many introverts are observant, focused listeners. Thus, you may notice ideas that others overlook. Take those ideas and consider how they may apply to your team or project. With your strong planning skills, you can make sure the changes you identify become reality, rather than remaining fleeting thoughts.

## Implementing Good Change

No matter where you fit in the four change patterns today, train yourself to be a change leader. While tolerators may begrudgingly roll with the changes, enthusiasts may be attracted to change for its own sake. Take a timeout to challenge the value of change. Many enthusiasts latch on to most any idea to help satisfy their need for and belief in change without testing its worth. Will this create the impact you are seeking? Will it be worth the turmoil that change can create? Over time, others will develop change fatigue if they are inundated with changes that either never get implemented or aren't providing the results once promised.

I once worked for a manager that literally would run out of his office once every week or two screaming: "Stop what you are doing! I have an idea. We are going to focus on something new." Yet a week or two later he would insist we ditch that last initiative because he had a better idea now. Be a change leader rather than an enthusiast. You are the idea generator that considers notions, seeks input, and champions those that will truly have a major impact on your business.

Introverts tend to take ideas and quickly develop them in our mind and implement them in our day. Stop. If you share your innovative ideas with a diverse group of co-workers, not only will your ideas be stronger, but they will also be much more inclusive. Ask for opinions. Seek out challenge. See if your colleagues or team members have their own ideas on how to solve the issues. It is not easy to stop your own momentum, but if you step back and invite diverse perspectives, others will take ownership in the changes before they are enacted. Don't skip this step. It is one of the hallmarks of true leaders and exceptional teams.

The way leaders process change is often what sets them apart. People that can handle the changes that are naturally thrust upon them are good team players. Those that seek and implement worthwhile change with their teams are unique, valuable, and sought-after leaders. These are not easy roles for anyone to play, but introverts are well equipped to excel. Lean on your skills of curiosity, thoughtfulness, creativity, and resiliency coupled with a focused mindset and you are well on your way!

## ACTIONS:

1. Would you consider yourself change resistant, change tolerant, a change enthusiast, or a change leader? What steps do you plan to take to improve your skill?

2. When changes occur, step back and calmly assess the situation and how you can best adapt.

Chapter Seven

# COMMUNICATION STARTS WITH YOU

*"We all need people who will give us feedback.*
*That's how we improve."*
*−Bill Gates, co-founder of Microsoft Corp,*
*global philanthropist (1955- )*

Calvin Coolidge, 30th US President, is considered by many to have been extremely introverted. He was even known as "Silent Cal." The story goes that at a presidential bash, one woman bet her friend she couldn't get the president to say three words to her. Her friend took the bet and approached Coolidge, laughingly explaining the wager. He stared right at her and sternly replied: "You lose!"

Even today, many believe introverts are people who do not like to speak or be sociable. While Coolidge may have been a man of few words, many introverts enjoy socializing and performing in public. Beyoncé, David Letterman, Lady Gaga, and Barack Obama help to dispel old myths. Introverts can be successful in any social situation or endeavor; they just have to do it their way.

It is easy to be awestruck or envious of the louder, more boisterous people in the middle of the crowd, those dominating a meeting, or others working the audience from the stage. However, as we've discovered, there are many ways to be a leader and they all start with being yourself. Communicating in the office during presentations, at meetings, or out networking should be done your own way. Build on your authenticity. Good interaction starts from within.

Remarkably, according to Lesley Sword of the Gifted Development Center, their study noted that "more than 75% of people with an IQ above 160 are introverted."[12] Our patient, introspective nature leads to balanced analysis and strong results. The key is to partner this intelligence with the communication skills to share this knowledge and make a difference.

In this chapter we will first refresh our mindset to overcome common introvert concerns about communication. We will then talk about how to use your strengths to succeed in four common communication forums: thinking on your feet, influencing others, presentations, and feedback. Finally, we will briefly cover how to achieve a "fit for purpose" mix of communication methods to be most effective. Your communication branch is essential to express yourself and contribute strength to your passions.

## Resetting your Mind

Reflection and preparation are common attributes for introverts like us. However, communicating with others is all about striking a balance—relaxing to let your true self shine through and then practicing in order to build self-confidence. Stop overthinking and shift your mindset to the topic or group you are with. If you allow, your natural curiosity will guide you through intriguing conversations.

## Dislodging Introvert's Paralysis

Past experiences of Introvert's Paralysis may instill fear of future disappointment and embarrassment. Introvert's Paralysis is when the mind just freezes up. We are unable to coherently communicate, whether in a one-on-one conversation, at a meeting table, or at a group speech or presentation. The mind goes blank and all the topics we prepared are temporarily wiped from our brain. We stand there in awkward silence, imploring ourselves to remember and say something.

This paralysis is often due to three different issues. First, there's anxiety about speaking at work or social events. We build up our apprehension and our thoughts swirl before the discussions even begin. It's like the clickety-clack of a roller coaster climbing up the first hill. The ride ahead may be fun, but for many that first ascent is torture. Secondly, we often over prepare to meet the challenge. We jot down notes for when it is our turn to introduce ourselves, or we memorize a position statement or a speech we are going to give. While leaning on preparation skills is natural and soothing, don't overdo it. It is impossible to relax and just converse when struggling to remember each note or line that we memorized. And if we forget something, the resulting stiffness and frustration can be debilitating. Thirdly, our paralysis is directly related to our level of self-confidence. While we can't simply wish for renewed confidence, we can practice with small steps like conversing with a friend or role modeling an upcoming meeting or speech with family. Implementing the Growth Rings Model to modestly stretch and grow will build our communication toolbox.

Though the thought of talking with others may overwhelm us at times, we need not worry. We talk with others all the time. Individuals tend to hold up famous people and TV characters as the standard, but we don't need to be a great orator or writer to communicate well with others. Instead of those seemingly polished people who often have Teleprompters and multiple takes, watch others around you. Several may have the gift of gab, but most everyone stammers a bit, pauses to gather their thoughts, or forgets a few points. They have their own style, as do you. You are no different from them. Besides, as Eleanor Roosevelt stated: "You wouldn't worry so much about what others think of you if you realized how seldom they do." What a great truth to lean on.

We must remind ourselves that Introvert's Paralysis is a fallacy. It's not because we *can't* communicate. Introvert's Paralysis is a combination of anxiety, over preparedness, and a lack of confidence and experience. Observing others and practicing various scenarios will chip away at the nerves and you will eventually find your flow.

## Perception is Reality

If you are like many introverts, you may be reserved, private by nature, and often deep in thought considering the many angles of an issue. You might prefer to concentrate on a project in your office or a private meeting room rather than amongst others. You may need to eat your lunch alone or go off campus for refueling time. These are all prudent steps for managing your energy level. Yet those around you who do not understand these needs may interpret your behavior as aloofness or a lack of interest to work as a team. I had more than one person in my career ask: "Why are you so aloof?" Others suspected I didn't want to socialize with them or, worse yet, didn't respect their diverse opinions or background. This was definitely not the image I was trying to put forth, but perception is reality.

It was up to me to correct that picture. I thought I had to do it by wearing my mask. It took me decades to realize the right way to dispel the view is not to discard my own personality, but to share it instead. The best medicine is to openly share your introversion with the team in your own authentic way. Such vulnerability will often gain you tremendous respect and empower you to speak your mind.

Embrace your authentic mindset and approach communication of all types with calmness. Lean on your strengths to <u>adequately</u> prepare for meetings from the one-on-one lunches to the large project team meetings covered in the next chapter. Communication starts with great listening skills, which provide us a platform to show care, thoughtfulness, and curiosity. Approach engagements as an opportunity to both quench your desire to learn as well as a chance to share expertise with others—this shifts your focus away from your own anxieties.

Maybe your communication skills are rusty. Reflect on our Growth Rings Model from Chapter 5 to practice and stretch yourself in small increments, with each ring representing a more diverse and unfamiliar audience. Each step strengthens your confidence in communicating authentically.

## How to Conquer Four Common Nemeses

You don't have to push yourself to be front-and-center in every conversation. Your introversion will likely guard against that. However, there are times when your expertise and ideas – indeed your voice – is needed. Regardless of whether you are a manager or not, leaders prove their value by navigating four key communication situations. Some may turn and hide, yet this is where you make a difference in the business and possibly in another person's career path. You have been called upon to lead. The good news is you already have the tools to do so.

## Thinking on Your Feet

You don't always have time to prepare in today's time-sensitive business world. An emergency or dangerous situation may present itself and you have to act quickly. Or someone challenges your assertions in a meeting or asks you for your opinion in a hallway conversation. Sometimes you can deflect, giving yourself the chance to process the question or challenge properly. That can be a perfectly acceptable option. However, other times you must join in the conversation.

This is why the information in the first section of this book is so critical. If you understand and practice how to exert your true self, your authenticity will shine when the spotlight is thrust upon you. If you haven't done your own work, then your response may be what you think others want to hear or simply a stab in the dark. Either way, these approaches are hard to defend and can lead to bad decisions. Small lies turn into big disasters. Personal agendas are quickly sniffed out. Any of these responses reveal a level of uncertainty others can detect.

Start with questions to better understand the situation and viable alternatives. Asking questions also provides you time to formulate your contributions. Tap your listening and thoughtfulness skills, as well as your values, to guide your responses. You can't go wrong if you are honest and lean on your own expertise and desire to do the right thing for your team and the company. Flexing your authenticity is always the right path. Others may not agree with your position, but they can at least respect your views and points, and so can you.

## Influencing Others

Life is often about influencing others—trying to guide your spouse, kids, manager, co-workers, or customers to understand a situation or opportunity the way you do in order to align your interests. Sometimes these discussions are simple and other times they may be quite complex, requiring weeks of team strategizing.

In either case, preparation and empathy will take you further than inciting conflict or trying to force compliance. Prepare by understanding the problem or opportunity, feasible options, your own strengths and weaknesses in the discussion, as well as those same factors for the other person. With this information, you will know what levers to pull, when to push, and when to step back.

Some discussions are transactional—a one-time activity without any lasting repercussions, like buying a car—but most are relational. In those cases, the issue under discussion contributes to a longer term personal or business relationship, so striving for a win-win solution is more important than claiming victory. Be sure both yourself and the other party recognize this context.

Lead with questions to best understand the dynamics. Follow with both parties sharing views and desires, and then focus on those items deemed critical to form an agreement. Be patient in working toward an accord. With appropriate preparation and consideration, you can feel confident as you seek to influence others in various situations.

# Presentations

Presentations, for our purpose here, are more formal, auditorium-style speeches than the small or medium-size meetings that are covered in the next chapter. While many people, especially shy ones, avoid these larger performances, many introverts thrive in presentations. They enjoy sharing their knowledge in a one-way conversation with a captive, attentive, and often faceless audience in a dark room.

However, for the less adventurous, speaking on a stage can be terrifying. Jay Artale, former Executive Director at Sony Pictures Home Entertainment, recalls: "[My] reaction to public speaking was abject fear, and physical reaction... over which I had no control. It was a form of powerlessness, and people who didn't have such fear had no concept of how debilitating it can be."

I certainly relate to Jay's sense of panic. Eventually, I realized my career goals would not let me avoid such presentations. I recognized that I could overcome my shyness and introverted tendencies through preparation, practice, and self-confidence.

Here are ten tips that will help manage the anxiety as well as the energy drain that even the most adventurous introvert must combat:

1. Develop and practice your presentation. Write the full speech down and read it frequently. Don't memorize, as this invites Introvert's Paralysis. As you gain familiarity, translate it to a bullet list—a high-level version of which you may have handy on a notecard or posted on slides for quick reference.

2. Check out the venue. Walking the room can help build a level of comfort and security.

3. Give yourself the gift of Positive Self Talk. It helps to put yourself in the right frame of mind and to envision a successful presentation.

4. Start with a question or bold statement to connect with the audience and pique their curiosity.

5. Smile and be enthusiastic. Even for the most serious of topics, people will connect with you more if they see you are enjoying yourself. High energy is contagious.

6. Slow down and enunciate. It's natural to talk quickly when nervous. Reminding yourself to slow down when you get started can do the trick.

7. Keep going. Remember, you are the only one who knows the speech as it was originally written. Don't worry if you skip points or ad lib words. Relax and your expertise will flow.

8. Practice self-compassion. Presentations are on the Frontier ring for many, so be proud of your courage. It's all about being impactful, not perfect. Revel in your success.

9. Find a nice warm, quiet place to re-energize afterward. Listen to music, read a book, grab a meal with close family or friends or by yourself. This is your reward for conquering the Frontier ring.

10. Jot down your own feedback. Start with what went well. Don't lose those highlights as you seek to identify areas to improve. Then note items you would like to enhance next time, whether that's the venue, the speech, audience engagement, or your own calmness. Be sure to capture the lessons that will make the next speech even more pleasant.

Use the Growth Ring Model for your presentation journey at work. If you are apprehensive, don't dive into large audiences but start with your Home Base (family) and reach to your Neighborhood (co-workers or friends) before stretching to strangers (Adventure) or leaping to your Frontier (larger audiences). It may take several attempts within a ring before you are ready to tackle the next one. And remember: it's not the destination, it's the journey. You may find large audience presentations are not your thing, but I guarantee that if you work through The Growth Model, you will build experience and confidence to expand your comfort zone and your pride no matter what ring you land on. Enjoy your journey!

## Feedback is a Gift

Our fourth method of communication is feedback. The best leaders are determined to offer constructive feedback and crave this gift themselves. Many introverts who value learning and reflection gravitate toward feedback. It is equally important to be both a provider of constructive criticism and a welcoming receiver of pointers and advice.

To receive comments well, you need to have the right mindset. Todd Miner, a senior advisor at a global Business Management Consultancy group, recalls: "It requires a level of self-confidence to accept [feedback] without being demoralized. It also requires a level of self-awareness." If you become defensive or immediately challenging, you will miss the nuggets of advice in all feedback. Curiosity and the drive for improvement will spur you to seek out these nuggets. Few people offer their comments voluntarily, because it can place them in an awkward situation if they don't know how you may react. After all, feedback can involve difficult, conflict-sparking conversations that may bruise someone's ego. In most cases, you must solicit feedback. Ask your manager, team members, and external customers/suppliers for their honest thoughts during projects or after meetings. People may be surprised by the request, but you can offer them time to reflect—a special gift to fellow introverts. Let them know you would like to follow up in a couple of days. Many companies also conduct annual anonymous feedback surveys for managers and occasionally for all staff members. This is a great time to collect information and identify themes worthy of your attention.

A best practice is to receive the feedback, write it down, thank the provider, and ponder it when you have time and are in the right mindset. You do not have to agree with all the comments, but you should consider them all before disqualifying any. Inevitably, you will discover at least a nugget or two of wisdom buried in even the most poorly phrased input. In addition to thanking the provider of the feedback after they share, go back to them later, thank them again, and share a couple of actions you have taken from their suggestions. Ask more questions if you want to delve deeper. Invite them to hold you accountable for the changes you are working on. What an empowering message this sends others. They will appreciate that you found value in their input and will be apt to provide further contributions another time. They will also be primed to receive feedback from you as well.

Feedback is not always easy to receive and can also be difficult to give. Ask others if they are open to feedback. Start by offering positive remarks regarding the meeting or your overall impression of their style and contributions before suggesting an area ripe for further development. Offering comments demonstrates empathy and compassion.

The feedback you receive can be an important catalyst for change and growth, both for you personally and for the business, but it is up to you how much you gather and how you use it. Consider it a gift worth asking for.

## Fit-for-Purpose Communication

To be most effective, select appropriate communication methods for different situations. There are many ways to communicate these days: electronically, on the phone, face-to-face, and via video calls like Zoom. In a 2020 poll of 140 members of various introvert Facebook groups, 74% favored text or email, 9% face-to-face, 4% on the phone, and 13% either simply replied "No, I don't communicate," or jested that their preference was either telepathically, through smoke signals, or via carrier pigeon. I think we can all relate to those responses. Courtney D. offered: "The phone is especially excruciating for me because I rely on visual cues to guide me through conversations. I hate it when we end up speaking at the same time on the phone and then there's an awkward silence and then we end up talking over each other again! Just email me or let's chat in person at a scheduled time." Everyone has their most comfortable method, but the key is not to rely entirely on your favorite and instead use each method with purpose. If we all only sent emails or only conducted face-to-face communications, we would surely be stressed and ineffective.

## Electronics

Most introverts rely on email or text for communication. It's easy to get our message out there, doesn't invite conflict, can be planned and reviewed before sending, and it's quick, so you can move on to the next task. However, emails and texts don't convey the whole story. You can't interpret other's emotions, convictions, or personal tone. Worse yet, emails can be misinterpreted. Emails are best used to share facts, reports, and appointments. Texts should be used even less in the business context, perhaps only as a quick reminder of something. Intracompany posting systems are becoming popular and help direct comments to targeted individuals or groups, yet you should still be cautious of overusing them at the expense of more personal communications.

## Phone

Whether one-on-one or group calls, the phone is often an introvert's nemesis. An incoming call screams for you to stop what you are doing and deal with an unexpected topic without any preparation. On top of that, a teleconference forces you to compete with others to get your questions or point across. There is no sense of body language or attitude that contributes to the dialogue or helps you to convey your message. Before you make a call, review the meeting tips shared in the next chapter to be most prepared. Also remember: you control your own time. There is no rule that you must answer all incoming calls. Let them roll to voicemail so you can continue whatever you were working on. Later, you can check voicemail and quickly prepare for a return call.

## Face-to-Face

This may not be your favorite way to communicate because it takes time, can foster conflict, and may include obligatory chitchat. However, face-to-face communication is critical, especially for any personal conversations, potentially contentious topics, and rapport building. The personal touch enables you to gather and convey emotion, determination, curiosity, and warmth, none of which are easily achieved over the phone or via email. The key to these conversations is to set a foundation. Building rapport early with your manager, team, co-workers, and critical stakeholders will pay dividends when issues arise, projects hit rough spots, or you are looking for an ally. Share your personal history and what you are working on to grease the skids so that future conversations are much smoother. If the conversation does become too chaotic or heated, you may certainly call a break to reconvene at another date, thus providing you with time to plan your next approach. You will find many more tips in the Networking chapter.

## Video/Zoom Calls

The Coronavirus pandemic certainly accelerated growth in video calls in 2020. People have adjusted to this new venue, and companies have continued to encourage remote work going forward. Thus, video calls are supplementing face-to-face meetings as well as many traditional phone calls. This can be a sweet spot for many introverts as they often combine the ability to prepare with the visual component that accommodates smooth interactions and rapport building. Don't limit these calls to just formal meetings—include Zoom coffees for one-on-one networking and pre-meeting strategizing. Be sure to log in early to tackle any unexpected technical issues. However, a few words of warning. Be cognizant that others are watching. Dress and act appropriately. Be mindful of your own body language and level of engagement that can be compromised if you are compelled to multi-task.

Using each communication tool appropriately and effectively will go a long way to building relationships and knowledge. Kayla W. from the introvert's Facebook survey summed it up nicely: "I love text as much as any introvert, especially since I can reread it. But it's also SO hard to understand tone and intention. So even though it may be uncomfortable, video and face-to-face are often better for me in the long run."

Certain people thrive in social situations and others prefer solitude. Yet we are all part of a dependent community at work and at home. Communication connects us. It solves problems, it conveys information, it shares feedback, and it makes life sweeter. You don't have to divert from your natural tendencies but be sure to use your strengths to get your voice into the room.

## ACTIONS:

1. What is your communication style? How can you use your strengths to become a more confident communicator? Seek to practice communications to build self-confidence.

2. Consider one opportunity to influence others, either at home or at work. Plan out your conversation, practice, and begin. Take pride in your efforts.

3. Be sure to ask for feedback after your next meeting or project. Carve out time to analyze the feedback in search of items you can change or improve.

4. Evaluate your communication mix. How can you most effectively use email, phone, face-to-face, and video calls to conduct business and develop stronger relationships?

## *The Corporate Introvert* – **Accompanying Worksheets**

Free Worksheets accompany most chapters so you can record your strengths, values, and passions and develop your own plan to apply your talents to become a confident and authentic leader.

https://www.BeyondIntroversion.com/tci-landing-page

Chapter Eight

# BECOMING
# A MEETING HERO

*"The important thing is to know what you know*
*and know what you don't know."*
*—Warren Buffett, American investor,*
*business tycoon, philanthropist (1930- )*

Meetings are an essential way of conveying information, creating alignment, and making decisions. They are a vital branch on your tree. We've all been a part of well-organized, purposeful meetings as well as wasteful, chaotic ones. Introvert leader Dr. Ty Belknap notes: "Meetings are the playground of extroverts." [13]

However, as Nick W. discovered: "I struggle performing in... endless meetings. I get through by preparing for these situations and ultimately producing high-quality results. As a creative, I find not many people have my skills in the corporate world, so my work is well respected." Nick has recognized how to lean on his own strengths to bring his voice into the room and shine.

This chapter focuses on how to create and participate in productive project meetings through proven checklists. Take advantage of the introvert's strengths: preparation, order, and learning. Tap into other strengths like empathy, resilience, and the creativity Nick referenced to excel at both leading and participating in meetings.

We will cover staff meetings in Chapter 15, Culture Creator.

## Leading a Productive Meeting

Leading a productive meeting is all about preparation. Better preparation generates greater confidence and consequently less anxiety. I suspect a lot of meeting apprehension starts from our school days when we had to recite a poem or present to the class on arcane subjects like Johannes Gutenberg's printing press. However, at work you are likely to be presenting on a topic that you are familiar with, if not the resident expert on. Focus on your mission to share your knowledge with others and to gather valuable insight and ideas to improve your project.

Meetings range from one-on-one or small group working sessions to large gatherings with formal procedures. All too often we jump straight into the meeting. Schedules are busy and we fail to prepare. The **READY-SET-GO-NEXT** checklist below serves to both calm your nerves and drive toward a most productive meeting.

# READY

- **Develop a specific objective.** Many meetings do not have an obvious purpose, especially recurring project meetings that are scheduled in perpetuity. As a meeting leader, ask yourself what is the true objective of this meeting? If the objective is not well defined and the material to support the meeting objective is still developing, cancel or delay the gathering. There is no shame in rescheduling a meeting. Everyone will appreciate your respect for their time and your intention to host a productive session.

- **Set a crisp agenda.** Put together a high-level agenda. Challenge yourself to ensure that each item has a purpose. What is the objective of each agenda item? Do you have the necessary information to achieve each objective, or should you delay specific items to a future meeting or handle in a smaller forum? Send out your draft agenda either to all attendees or to a small group to solicit input. Are you missing any important topics? Do others question why certain items are on the agenda? Is the ordering of topics creating a logical flow? Once you have input, finalize the agenda, and distribute at least a couple of days in advance.

- **Select meeting time and place.** As the organizer, consider the time and place of your meeting. Mid-morning tends to bring the most energy. Meetings over lunch may provide the best attendance, but you should allocate extra time, as attendees will be pre-occupied with mealtime socializing. Late day meetings can find a drained group counting down the minutes left in a long day.

  You should also ponder the location. Challenge yourself to consider non-traditional venues. Meetings no longer have to take place in stodgy rectangular rooms. Try an outdoor location, a stand-up meeting, or even a walking conversation for small groups of two or three. These can keep the energy up and spark needed creativity as well.

- **Invite only value-added attendees.** Meeting organizers tend to invite people for various reasons. Some attendees bring critical information while others have worked hard on aspects of the project or are vital decision makers. Others may be allies there for moral support or co-workers attending for a broadening experience. Before you know it, the room will be overflowing, and the cumulative amount of staff time becomes eye opening. Generally, larger meetings are less efficient as everyone is tempted to chime in and add their personal agendas. Identify the critical players——those bringing information vital to the stated objective. Some may be reluctant to attend while others may be concerned about being omitted. Start by explaining the meeting objective, perhaps agreeing that sharing pre-read and meeting notes will suffice for those not considered critical. This will trim the attendees and ensure those that do attend will be there voluntarily, ready to actively participate rather than mumbling their displeasure from the back row.

## SET

- **Gain alignment before the meeting.** This pre-work is perhaps the most important differentiator toward a successful meeting. Once you've identified invitees, spend time evaluating each. Which attendees may be considered allies on this project, and which may be doubters? Anticipate potential roadblocks to a successful meeting. Invest time through informal huddles with skeptics. The primary goal here is to diffuse potential conflict and gain alignment. Listen to their positions and rationale and share your own. Consider what other agendas may be at play. Ideally, you can remove any challenges or table those agendas for another meeting. At the minimum, seek to build mutual respect and lay the groundwork for civil dialogue within your session's objectives.

- **Consider the personalities in the room.** Are there any intimidating people joining? Certain personalities tend to halt conversation. People stop sharing and bow to the daunting figure. Consider meeting with this person in advance to share meeting objectives. You may subtly emphasize the importance of getting input from all key decision makers and that the meeting will have to move swiftly to achieve that objective. You may also consider enlisting your manager or a senior ally to neutralize this issue if it develops during the meeting.

- **Issue pre-read.** For extensive or intensive meetings, consider sending background material with the agenda so the meeting will be more productive. Pose questions in the pre-read note so attendees can consider their contributions to the discussion. Introverts will especially appreciate this addition, as it eases the burden of thinking on the fly.

- **Prepare and practice your topic.** While a meeting is not an oratory contest, you want to be well versed on your subject and prepared for a smooth presentation to keep the focus on the agenda. You can refer to notes or PowerPoint slides during the meeting, but avoid reading verbatim so you don't lose engagement with the participants. Don't try to memorize the presentation. When you share your topic, it will surely be different than the speech you practiced. Words will change, stories will be different, items may be forgotten, and other items may be interjected. You will be the only one to know the difference. It is more important to have a grasp of the facts and be flexible and engaging in the conversation. You have a message to share that the audience wants to hear.

# GO

- **Create an inclusive atmosphere.** Your role is not to dictate the meeting, but to guide the forum toward a productive conclusion with broad input from everyone. Who may be shy or introverted, perhaps needing additional attention to coax their input? Our Leadership Quiz indicates introverts are three times more apt to be involved when called upon, rather than initiating their own input. Simply asking their opinion during the meeting can create an opening for sharing. Rather than enlisting a roundtable brainstorming session that puts everyone under the spotlight, consider providing Post-It notes and a few minutes for everyone to gather their thoughts before sharing on a particular topic. Most participants will appreciate this approach and the quality of the input will be noticeably improved. Others may be quite talkative, perhaps necessitating efforts to keep them in check. Don't hesitate to tactfully ask them to pause as you enlist other opinions in the room. The leader's role is to balance the brainstorming, reactive responses, and thoughtful consideration in order to gain diverse views around the table.

   Sometimes information is revealed that might derail the meeting. If there are well-founded reasons to adjust the agenda midstream, be flexible and acknowledge the information or perspective. Determine if it's best to modify the agenda on the fly or reschedule. Many introverts find it quite challenging to relinquish control and execution of a well-conceived plan.

However, being mindful that a pause to ensure objectives are met in the long term may be a prudent approach. As we discussed in an earlier chapter, don't fight the change but advocate for it when it appears wise.

- **Be concise.** Rarely do people need all the details and background about a subject. In your preparation, familiarize yourself with the key value drivers and the points that are most important to be brought into the room for consideration. Share those with crispness and confidence. Then scan the room and ask for questions. Rather than droning on about a subject hoping to hit everyone's concerns, their questions will point you exactly to what needs to be addressed. Once the questions are exhausted, you are done.

I once came to a meeting with twenty slides supporting a proposal I was soliciting. After two slides, the leader pronounced his agreement and polled the others gaining their concurrence. I looked at my manager for guidance and he flashed his hand across his throat and gave me a thumbs-up. The objective of the meeting was not to share twenty slides, but to gain support. With that accomplished, the meeting was happily closed.

# NEXT

- **Follow up promptly after the meeting.** Craft a succinct recap including actions with identified owners and agreed-upon delivery dates. Issue the notes promptly and provide a window for any comments. Once that deadline passes, distribute the final notes. Be sure to place your actions in your calendar or planner. Finally, carve out time to review how the meeting went with key participants. What went well? What could have been improved? Did you skip any of these steps? Such a review is the mark of a strong leader and will help you continue to improve your meeting leadership skills.

For introverts, ample preparation reduces anxiety and leaves them more in control and relaxed to guide productive, inclusive meeting discussions.

## Being a Valuable Meeting Participant

If you're introverted, you may find attending meetings to be nerve-racking. Many involve unfamiliar topics and people expect you to speak up amidst a strange conglomeration of attendees. As a participant, you have been invited because you have unique information critical to the meeting. Don't try to play the game of the competitive meeting player jockeying for airtime without delivering true value. Instead, lean on your skills of preparation, listening, and resilience to selectively participate. Be sure to prepare yourself in advance by applying our **READY-SET-GO-NEXT** process:

## READY

- **Confirm or challenge your attendance.** Cherish your time and defend it as the key to your productivity. As an introvert, it's important to maintain control over your calendar as much as possible. Meetings provide a perfect opportunity to practice this mantra. Most organizations have too many aimless meetings. Understand specifically why you have been invited. Are you a subject matter expert presenting certain data, or you are attending because the project or decision may directly impact your business? As a meeting invitee, be on the lookout for sessions that don't have a clear objective. If your role is not obvious in the meeting, challenge your attendance with the organizer. A compromise might be to request to review pre-read and meeting notes with the promise to revert if you have any comments or questions. In my experience, filtering meetings often reduces your attendance by 10-20%, thus returning valuable time to your calendar.

- **Review the meeting agenda and pre-read.** Ask the organizer to provide an agenda and pre-read. Once you receive the material, jot down notes about key items you support and others you may question or oppose, so you are prepared to challenge with facts. Put asterisks next to major points you need to make. Consider huddling with the meeting host in advance so they are prepared to address any issues. Create time on your calendar for thorough preparation. Remember, you are not only a participant for the meeting agenda, but also a team representative that needs to understand the broader impact of the topic for your business.

## SET

- **Be present early.** Arriving early to get the lay of the land will help you feel more comfortable, as will a few handshakes or idle chitchat before the meeting begins. Stake out an appropriate spot at the meeting table. You don't need to jostle for a power position such as at the head of the table, but you also shouldn't be sitting in the back or on the periphery as this will degrade your authority and make it more difficult for you to actively participate. Contributing even a quick remark early in the meeting will help break the ice and get you into the flow. The longer you wait, the harder it will be to actively participate.

- **Observe the room.** Who's comfortable and who's not? What alliances have formed in the room? People may say one thing, but their body language may show disagreement, passion, anger, disappointment, or anxiety. Utilize a common introvert trait and pick up on these during the meeting and be cognizant of your own body language. If you sit with your arms crossed and a growl on your face, others will assume you are frustrated. That's fine if you want to convey your displeasure, but otherwise it is misleading and can be discouraging, especially to the leader.

# GO

- **Participate.** This doesn't mean you need to be argumentative, the most active voice, or the loudest in the room. Participate authentically. Participation involves listening, connecting points that others may gloss over, and then speaking when you have important data, observations, or recommendations to share.

  Sometimes it's especially difficult to get a word in amongst the more vociferous attendees. Make eye contact with the leader, jump in to confirm the last topic, and then add your viewpoint. Raise your hand if you can't find a pause in the conversation. You accepted an invitation because you have expertise or perspective that you and others want in that room. Use your notes, prepared questions, and highlighted issues. Be respectful of the contributions of others but do not allow them to neglect your efforts to join the conversation.

  If you have a fleeting thought spurred on by the meeting discussions, jot it down and then redirect your attention back to the meeting. Your primary role is to listen so you can also be prepared to jump in when appropriate.

If you are unable to answer a question, rather than ramble, speculate, or lie, indicate you need time to research and that you will then report back. The way you handle these situations can either reinforce your reputation or destroy your credibility. People respect the need to evaluate items without taking up everyone's valuable time. Just be sure to get back to the meeting leader or participants with your findings.

- **Be a team player.** While you are representing your work or team, you are also a valued member of the project team itself. Use your tact to both support and challenge statements and offer your opinion. If you anticipate conflict based on the pre-read, touch base with the meeting organizer in advance to find an amiable solution that progresses the agenda.

## NEXT

- **Take action notes.** Focus your time on the discussions at hand rather than taking copious notes. However, be sure to capture specific decisions and your assigned actions. Share pertinent information with your teammates and manager.

- **Place your actions in your daily planner.** This helps relieve anxiety of missed obligations and lets you plan for proper follow through. This step is often forgotten, but lost actions and lack of follow up are not forgotten. Your success and reputation depend upon it.

## Keys to Smooth Zoom Calls

The growth of remote meetings like Zoom exploded during the COVID crisis and continues to grow as cost management and work/life balance align to encourage virtual working arrangements. The steps above still apply, but you may need to be more creative to accomplish them virtually. In addition to highlights regarding Zoom calls in the Communication chapter, here are key reminders:

- Technical issues suggest the leader test connections by logging on at least ten minutes early. Participants should be encouraged to do the same.

- Leaders should set ground rules to keep everyone focused and to ensure full inclusivity during the meeting.

- Participants need to avoid the temptation to multi-task during calls so they can be fully engaged.

- Rapport is harder to build online, especially in large meetings, so seek pre-meeting virtual coffees or breakout sessions to lay the groundwork.

- Because it is hard to get cues from the room, transitions amongst attendees are often difficult. Reserved participants tend to be quieter, and extroverts are often louder and more long-winded on virtual calls. The leader needs to observe with a keen eye and guide the room.

- Periodically survey everyone to see if they would like to add to the discussion and to ensure agreement of actions and decisions at the end.

Meetings are a critical work event. A cross-section of teams or organizations comes together to achieve specific objectives. How you prepare and execute your role will go a long way in achieving work goals and establishing your reputation. That may seem like a heavy weight to place on yourself, but by leveraging your strengths of preparation, learning, thoughtfulness and resilience, your own style will help you excel.

## ACTIONS:

1. When you are a meeting conductor, review the READY-SET-GO-NEXT steps above and be prepared to lead.

2. When you are a meeting participant, review the READY-SET-GO-NEXT steps above and ensure you arrive prepared.

3. Evaluate your remote meetings to develop the rapport and effectiveness of in-person sessions.

4. Observe other meeting leaders and participants to see what appears to work well and what doesn't, and decide if you would like to incorporate any of their techniques into your own style.

*The Corporate Introvert*

# Chapter Nine

# NETWORKING YOUR WAY

*"Instead of building walls, we can help build bridges."*
*—Mark Zuckerberg, co-founder and CEO of Facebook*

Networking. The word often leaves a bad taste in introverts' mouths. Why do we need to network anyway? Can't we just skip it?

Even the most solitary jobs have a component of engagement with co-workers, managers, or counterparties. You will interact with team members, collaborate with other groups, negotiate with suppliers and customers, and job search with managers and resource holders. This is how we survive within the corporate community. Networking is a prominent branch of our tree, so let's discover how we can make it strong and supportive. We will explore how you are already networking and how you can be prepared to excel at networking your way.

## Networking Authentically

Networking seems so social and extroverted that it can turn us introverts off. But before we spiral down this stereotype, let's step back for a minute and tackle the idea of sociability. Introverts are social! We talk with our family, friends, and co-workers, and generally enjoy it. We then try to recharge afterwards in our own way. This is the true definition of a sociable introvert.

If we dissect those pleasant social interactions, we often find they are with familiar people, often in familiar places, for shorter durations, covering interesting topics. Those attributes define a comfortable social networking approach for us. In fact, these dynamics may give us an advantage over more extroverted partygoers since people tend to develop closer relations and tighter bonds in one-on-one situations. So rather than feel compelled to join a room full of strangers, we need to rely on our strengths to make this branch of our tree comfortable and strong.

**Familiar people**: Start with people you already know—teammates, co-workers, and customers you talk to on the phone and via email. Deepen these relationships through coffees and lunches. This practice builds confidence as you widen your network later.

**Familiar places**: There is value in home-field advantage. Host meetings in your office, suggest a walking meeting, or arrange a meal at a favorite restaurant.

**Shorter duration**: Lengthy networking events can be especially exhausting, even with your closest family or friends. Plan accordingly.

**Interesting topics**: Come prepared with personal and work topics such as vacation plans and a favorite hobby, as well as your current project or work problem. Consider what you already know or are curious to learn about your networking partner and prepare questions to get the ball rolling.

Finally, I would add the sage advice of Karen Wickre, author of *Taking the Work out of Networking: An Introvert's Guide to Making Connections That Count*, who suggests: "This is my guiding principle for no-pressure networking: nurture it before you need it."[14] Develop rapport before a negotiation begins, issues arise, or a job search commences. Being proactive takes the pressure off networking and builds a platform for more collaborative work and better results later.

The key is to network authentically. Don't try to do what everyone else does. Use your strengths of thoughtfulness, learning, and preparation to network *your* way. If you evaluate your current friendships, they are strengthened by your willingness to be vulnerable, along with your curiosity and empathy for others. In doing so, you discover common interests and forge bonds that range from casual acquaintances to lifelong friendships. These are the same skills to lean on as you endeavor to expand your circle at work.

## Stretching Your Comfort Zone

Certainly, you cannot limit your networking to close family, friends, or co-workers. This is especially true when you are in a new assignment, with unfamiliar teammates and industry counterparts. Don't be envious or intimidated by the blossoming network of the gregarious socialite or of the extensive networks of entrenched co-workers. Yours is a patient game. Introverts grow relations one at a time. As you build experience and confidence, you will expand your circle further. Once you develop a base network, the challenge gets more manageable. Soon you will have friends to

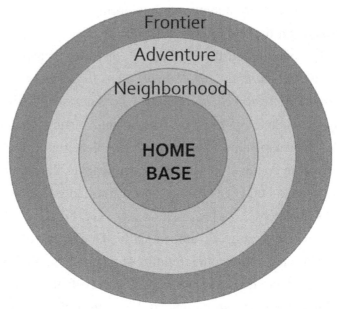

talk to, confidantes at work, and external contacts to engage with at events.

To build your networking bravado, let's return to the Growth Rings Model introduced in Chapter 5 to illustrate how to stretch your comfort zone.

Your **Home Base** is your existing group of family and social friends. For many introverts, this tends to be a rather small group who you feel comfortable spending time with and sharing personal stories and common interests.

Your **Neighborhood** ring includes teammates and co-workers that you see most every day. Some may feel like family and others quite removed. This is a perfect opportunity to develop your skills in a safe environment. Grab a coffee or lunch. You may start with discussions about the team or work issues before broadening to queries about family, hobbies, travel, or career experiences and ambitions. You shouldn't expect to hit it off with everyone to the same degree, but the experience itself will build your social skills and confidence.

The **Adventure** ring involves company acquaintances. They may be co-workers on a project or people you see in the cafeteria, at training sessions, or in cultural groups. They may be managers in teams you are curious about or even your own manager. Yet the same tactics can still apply through one-on-one huddles. You can even conduct advanced research through LinkedIn to understand their background and identify common interests. You may strike up a friendship that leads to routine catch-ups, while others may remain on the level of exchanging casual "hellos" and nods in the hallway going forward. It's a perfectly natural funneling process to find those with whom you feel comfortable to be yourself while you develop a common bond together.

Certain Adventure relationships may be more formal, including role models, mentors, or sponsors. Role models are people you observe, perhaps without them even knowing it, to pick up examples of skills you may want to replicate. Mentors provide guidance and a sounding board to help you figure out work issues and career paths. Sponsors are people in your company or industry that know you and your work well. They can be extremely helpful in providing you with strong references, job leads, and career paths.

The final step is the **Frontier** ring. Interactions here are typically with industry cohorts. Certain jobs may offer few occasions to mingle within the industry while other roles depend on these relationships to conduct business. In either case, follow the same guidelines that you've used for your co-workers in the Neighborhood and Adventure rings. Leverage LinkedIn and other social media to mine for connections and prepare for initial meetings. Perhaps few of these relationships develop into social friendships, but the rapport you build will make your work more pleasant and may provide you with insights to help your business transactions in the future. Many long-term business deals or joint ventures happen in part because each company has products or services that the other company values, but most develop simply because of the camaraderie that arises from casual meals and discussions between counterparts.

Regardless of which ring you reside in, be sure to practice self-compassion and positive reinforcement. You may stretch to the Frontier or find that the Neighborhood or Adventure ring brings you maximum joy. You may end up with dozens of new contacts or a few strong friends. Your success is in the journey, not in the destination. Celebrate each ring and the courage to stretch your comfort zone. If you practice these steps with patience and compassion, you will own a stronger sense of self-esteem. If your job requires you to reach beyond your comfort, give it a try. However, if you conclude that activity remains anxiety inducing, consider changing positions so you can exchange the undue stress for a more rewarding job.

## Networking Tips for Large Events

Meeting unfamiliar people, especially in large settings like conferences and cocktail hours, can be nerve-racking for the most sociable of individuals and traumatic for the shyest introvert. Many of us are afraid our performance will be sloppy, unsuccessful, or embarrassing. We get too tied up in our heads trying to think about what we are going to say or recalling how awkward our last social call might have been. Sara Bonario shares: "These events or large gatherings where I don't know anyone... become overwhelming for me. I feel lost. Often people are facing each other in little circles and it is awkward... to nudge my way in."

Who says you have to go to conferences and work a room full of hundreds of strangers for hours? Your manager? Don't you think he really meant for you to go to an industry outing and develop some relationships and do some business? That's more like it. He probably didn't intend to be prescriptive—he just shared his approach, and that of many extroverts with expansive networks. You can still succeed at these events, but you'll want to modify your approach.

Return to your strengths and arrange one-on-one or small group meetings or meals during the conference with people you already know from your daily activity. Invite a friendly teammate along to help share the social burden. Prepare for each meeting and suddenly, you have the makings of a successful event without all the drama. You may also choose to arrange meetings before the gathering with new contacts, thus avoiding the more awkward introduction at the larger social events.

You may still join the cocktail hours to test yourself on the Frontier ring, so these tips may be especially helpful on that journey:

1.  **Know Yourself:** Remind yourself of your roots. Your talents of preparation, thoughtfulness, and learning will shine in networking. Don't let a typically more conservative tone at business events hinder you from sharing personal stories, asking about family, and showing empathy. Some may find such an approach unconventional, but many will quickly appreciate your personal style and passion. Use your curiosity to approach any conversation with an inquisitive tone. What can you learn about this person or their job that can help you

understand your business better? Leaning into your strengths is the most powerful way to conquer your apprehensions.

2. **Envision Success:** Review mindset methods from Chapter 4 to get in the proper frame of mind. Don't try to become the perfect orator or socialite. In fact, for many of us, initial awkwardness may be unavoidable. Don't beat yourself up. This helps make you unique. Confidence in your authenticity will be welcomed by others and calm your nerves in the process. You may even start by introducing yourself as an introvert or saying that you don't normally enjoy these events but that you really want to meet others and are curious about their stories. This approach of recognizing the elephant in the room often lightens the conversation, especially for the other introverts at the table. Take a deep breath. Life will go on after the meeting, cocktail, or party.

3. **Know Your Network:** Review your network before events. This doesn't need to be anything fancy, just a spreadsheet, a notebook, an app, or your LinkedIn list of friends. You'll be pleasantly surprised how often this information comes in handy when you want to prepare for a lunch or cocktail with past connections, or even when you are searching for your next job.

4. **Plan Your Targets:** Review the invitation list in advance. Identify people you would like to meet, or perhaps those you would like to avoid. You may know some attendees through work emails or phone calls. If so, plan to meet either at the event or in advance. Check out their LinkedIn or other social media to mine for common interests and introductory topics while developing your target list.

5. **Set Realistic Goals:** Before the event, set realistic goals. You don't need to stay for the entire cocktail party. You don't need

to build bonding relationships with everyone around the table. Maybe you commit to staying for one hour or to develop at least one relationship you can follow up with later. Once you accomplish that, you can give yourself permission to stay longer if you are feeling adventurous or leave with a feeling of accomplishment. Every small success builds on itself.

6. **Enlist a Buddy:** Consider pairing up with a co-worker, friend, or an external contact that is also unacquainted with the industry to work the room together. This will immediately help reduce your anxiety.

7. **Prepare Your List of Four:** We are all generally friendly and interesting people. Yet when overwhelmed, our minds can go blank, in an experience I described as Introvert's Paralysis in Chapter 7. Though introverts often feel more comfortable with meatier topics than chitchat, most conversations open with small talk. To prepare for the chatter, develop your List of Four. Put them together, practice them, bring them with you for reference in the corner or at a restroom break, and update them periodically:

   • **Questions for Strangers:** Start by asking questions which demonstrate your interest and help you identify people you may want to get to know better based on their responses. Ask about their hobbies or trips. Rather than ask, "What do you do?", ask what projects they are working on, what attracted them to their job, or what the biggest challenge is in their job.

   • **Interesting Points About You:** Prepare a list of your unique trips, hobbies, talents, passions, and dreams. These topics can be especially ripe if your research reveals your networking partner has similar interests. You should be able to free flow with this discussion.

- **Current Event Topics:** Scan the news for interesting items ranging from weather, sports, space programs, or history. Topics associated with your hobbies and interests are perfect lead-ins. The cardinal rule to avoid politics and religion remains sage advice.

- **Work Items:** Depending on the audience, you can inject your elevator speech of what you do, three projects you are working on, the biggest challenges in your job, or information you are seeking from your counterpart.

It may feel awkward to blurt out a question or share your vacation plans, but that unease is quickly forgotten. Once the conversation starts rolling, flex your listening skills to show interest and genuine empathy. After a few light introductory topics, feel free to get more in depth with those that appear engaged.

8. **Start Early:** I've always found if I show up early to a cocktail party and introduce myself to the few already there, my cluttered mind is distracted, and the butterflies disappear. Jumping into a crowded conversation can be an uncomfortable beginning to the night. Don't interrupt others' intense conversations. Search for more relaxed trios to join so you can pair up for discussions after the introductions. Use the questions from your List of Four to get started. I'm historically bad at names, so I try to pay particular attention and use names in a few sentences right away to help remember.

9. **Monitor Your Energy Gauge:** Provide yourself personal time in advance of the event to build your energy. During the event, as you feel your vigor plummeting, take a walk or duck into the restroom. Even just a few minutes can help refuel for the next conversation. Limit your alcohol intake. Grabbing drinks throughout the night might sound like a good way to relax your

inhibitions, but it often clutters all your plans and raises the risk of an embarrassing moment.

10. **Give Yourself a Break:** Remember, it takes two to have an interesting conversation and develop a bond. Some conversations go nowhere quickly and others are immediate connections. Most are somewhere in the middle, taking effort to explore the relationship before a spark is lit or the hot embers smolder. If a connection is obviously not there, feel free to exit rather than waste your time and energy. To avoid the awkward exit, you can either announce you are headed to the bar or buffet or that you would like to canvas the room before you must leave.

Don't let networking intimidate you. Your objective is not to become an extrovert or anyone you are not. Consider it an opportunity to share your stories and talents and extend your curiosity toward others, some of whom may become your most friendly or valuable connections. Networking can enhance your work experience and boost your self-confidence if you approach it in a genuine way.

At this point in the book, you have explored your roots and applied them to build a strong trunk and branches. You are equipped to succeed in the workplace without sacrificing your authenticity or happiness.

Take some time periodically to prune your branches by learning from mistakes, consolidating your efforts, and prioritizing your focus. Pruning will help you continue to grow stronger. Also be sure to enjoy the fruits of your labor—tie a hammock from your trunk to another, hang a swing on your branches. Don't worry, your tree is sturdy and reliable now, and you deserve the opportunity to bask in the sun's warmth from your splendid tree.

## ACTIONS:

1. Develop your List of Four and jot it down on an index card for your next event.

2. Setup/update a method for knowing your network.

3. Identify prospective role models, mentors, and sponsors to build your career development network.

4. Schedule at least one informal coffee or lunch meeting every couple of weeks.

# SECTION III:

# REACHING FOR THE SKY

Your superpowers provide you with the strength, conviction, and motivation to overcome traditional obstacles described in the last section. Section III focuses on fostering a partnership with your manager and creating the right fit for your growth and satisfaction.

If you stroll around your favorite park, you will likely see many trees angling around others to ensure they get adequate sunlight to expand and blossom. Much the same, employees need to ensure their environment is conducive for growth. Sometimes, this requires flexibility to bend around obstacles in order to create the best work environment. Other times, you may find the impediments too formidable and opt to move your tree elsewhere so you can grow and flourish.

Chapter 10 focuses on how to create a positive working relationship with managers. Your supervisors are the most important connections during your career. They have power over your work tasks, work/life balance, team culture, and your career development.

Introverts often feel pigeonholed into specific jobs. In Chapter 11, we examine the various types of roles available so you can consider how your strengths may apply to particular positions and form productive fits during your career.

Supervisory relationships and career management should not be one-way streets. Equipped with your strong roots and branches, you can now ensure you have ample sunlight to support your passions and dreams throughout your career.

Chapter Ten

# YOUR MOST IMPORTANT WORK RELATIONSHIP

*"Work for someone who believes in you,*
*because when they believe in you they'll invest in you."*
*—Marissa Mayer, American businesswomen and*
*former CEO of Yahoo!*

You will have many important relationships in your career, including direct reports, co-workers, and customers. Undoubtedly, the most critical work bond you will have is with your manager. Besides hiring you, this person will be in a position to support, challenge, train, recognize, promote, and fire you. You will likely work with well over a dozen managers during your career, so it's prudent to adopt a systematic approach to developing a productive relationship.

Many employees, especially introverts, do not feel empowered to play a joint role in the relationship with their manager. Instead, they are prepared to only take orders and vent frustrations once they return home. However, the association with your manager is a partnership, relying on both of you to communicate, share, and support each other. Ideally, you are in a role that fits your strengths and passions with a manager who values your input and collaboration. Foster this relationship from the start.

## Laying the Groundwork

Striking up personal conversations is often awkward. Managers may be reticent to create personal connections at work. Initially, this may come as a relief to introverts, but stretching yourself to establish this essential relationship will pay dividends. Gauge your manager's style and comfort. Perhaps a casual breakfast or lunch or time outside of work will be most conducive. Don't push these conversations but recognize when your manager appears ready.

Spend quality time with your manager focusing on how you can help deliver company goals. What is their vision of the team and your job in particular? Where does she want to see the team in a few years? Ask questions about her expectations, leadership style, and communication preferences. Then discuss your personal career objectives and what you are aiming to bring to and take from this job.

This relationship building is a critical investment for the future. Creating open dialogue with your manager early on makes further conversations, especially addressing business and career issues, much easier.

## Extending Your Model

As you work to build rapport with your managers, employ the same approach with your co-workers. Everyone has a role to play, and anyone could become your confidante, ally, or invaluable colleague. Get to know your teammates. Ask about work background, job tasks, and personal history.

Consider the other person's strengths or weaknesses. Do they seem open to sharing in these discussions? Do they appear humble, overconfident, or a wet noodle? It takes time to build trust, but you can often sense if you two will hit it off in the first few minutes. Remember, even if you don't feel compatible, they may still have a lot to contribute.

Sense if someone may be an ally or foe. Allies are those you can envision working closely with, confiding in, asking questions about team dynamics, and sharing work tips and hazards with. Foes are those who you may not get along with or who appear to be threatened by your presence in the group. Every team harbors hidden agendas, and it takes time to unveil them. Maybe someone has a cold, hard exterior, but that isn't who they are deep down inside. Assume the best in people and recognize that everyone is different.

Like many introverts, certain people warm up slowly and are less giving. This does not make them any less interesting or helpful. Don't give up on these relationships, and certainly don't go on the attack. It may be helpful to try other tactics, like one-on-one discussions, appealing to their expertise to try to neutralize them, or approaching them to request their help. A former foe may become your strongest ally. In either case, spend time with each team member. Make the connection and share your authentic self.

## The Elephant in the Room

For introverts, the "elephant in the room" is sharing your introversion. In our Leadership Quiz, only 52% of respondents have made this bold step. Such a declaration is courageous and it will alleviate years of personal turmoil. Many that resolve to hide their introversion suffer from low self-esteem because hiding their true self makes them feel unworthy. Others experience anxiety or depression, which can surface further as physical ailments like rashes, sciatica, shingles, or high blood pressure. Revealing your introversion opens the door for you to share your authentic self. You can make valuable contributions to business discussions seeking diverse input. You can become a role model for the "hidden half," the portion of employees in the workplace who are compelled to exist under the radar.

Doug Conant, former Campbell Soup CEO, implored: " One of the best ways I've found to help people overcome their discomfort around my behavior is to simply declare myself."[15] Openly discussing your introversion early in your career paves a positive path for you. If you weren't prepared to make such a statement years ago, it is never too late to share your personal journey. This doesn't mean making a speech in front of hundreds. Start with a close friend at work. Share at a routine one-on-one or annual review discussion or at a casual coffee with your manager. Relieve the weight from your shoulders and get your voice in the room. Your organization will pay homage to your courage—a quality many companies are lacking in this competitive business world.

Matt Kingsolver, a mid-level finance manager, shared: "I had a great feedback session with [my] business manager. I had the opportunity to tell him I consider myself an introvert. He found that really helpful and said it helped 'explain a lot.' We had a good chat and it... opened the door for an honest and helpful conversation." Being vulnerable with others can spark strong rapport while building your pride and confidence.

Once you have crossed this threshold, speaking through your strengths will become much easier and more natural. With renewed self-confidence, the support of your team, and continuous practice, communicating with others will be a pleasant extension of yourself. You don't have to wear a mask all day long.

## Scratching Below the Surface

When building a strong bond between two people, curiosity, respect, and vulnerability certainly help. Once you establish rapport, it is time to cultivate your alignment further. As you do, probe for more insights about your manager's style and how you can best work well together. Focus on four different areas:

1. **What are your manager's goals, as provided by their manager?** Presumably your goals cascade from these. If you are aware of these goals, you can support your manager by helping them meet or exceed their targets. You can also be on the lookout for any opportunities or risks that may affect your manager's plans.

2. **What is your manager's leadership style?** Managers can be hands-on or distant. Some delegate according to your skills or interests and others may be oblivious to such traits. Some seek constructive feedback while others only seek confirmation of their own approach. Managers lead in a variety of ways. Your styles may match, or they may be quite different. Understand this landscape and try to bridge differences from the start. You may have to bend to make the relationship work and flourish.

3. **What is your manager's communication style?** Would she rather have too much information and frequent updates or less of both? Does she prefer face-to-face conversations or emails? How often would she like to touch base?

4. **How does your manager plan to support your development?** Besides training you for this particular position, is your manager interested in discussing your career vision? Many managers and employees tend to defer this discussion, given the immediate need to get you up to speed on the job at hand. However, sharing career ambitions will help her support your plans by giving you projects or networking opportunities that build important bridges for your future.

Gauge your manager's manner and approachability. Will she be quite happy to answer these questions? You may need to observe her closely to sense her style.

## Assess Your Manager's Personality

People are much more complex than one simple label. However, considering where your manager may lie on the introversion/ extroversion spectrum will help gauge your approach and coordination. So where on this continuum do you believe your manager lies?

## My Manager is an Introvert

As an introvert, you may cheer this discovery. She will certainly understand you, your strengths, and your triggers. You may build wonderful rapport and walk hand-in-hand down the hallways. But it may not be so simple. If your manager is more of a thinker than a talker, it may be hard to tell what is on her mind. She may be reticent to share information or recognition, not because it isn't justified but because that's not a natural compulsion. Your manager may be a driven learner, wanting to understand history and details. As someone who may share a penchant for learning, be patient in answering a wide range of questions and providing details and data to quench her thirst for knowledge.

The best way to seek alignment is to communicate through a myriad of environments, from an office meeting to a casual work conversation or an informal coffee or lunch. Sharing your own vulnerability may entice your manager to share as well. As you reveal how your introverted personality has helped you learn, grow, and contribute at work, she may relate to your strengths and to your challenges as well. Perhaps you will form an unspoken bond to help each other out. Regardless, you have put this relationship on steady, respectful ground.

## My Manager is an Extrovert

As you discover that your manager may be more of a sociable, quick thinker, your heart might sink, but do not fear. Here again, I advocate having a variety of exchanges. Although you are not the most gregarious, off-the-cuff debater, offer positive experiences where you worked closely with a wide range of personality types. Share your definition of introversion as it relates to the Energy Equation and dispel myths. Regardless of differences in style, you may find this disparity is quite complementary. The key is to respect each other's approach and to leverage each other's strengths. This will deliver against your objectives and the team's as well. Introverts often find they have better relationships with extroverts, perhaps because they are natural conversation starters, minimize uncomfortable pauses, and place less pressure on us while we process discussions and ponder questions. Remain curious and open-minded.

## Align on a Communication Plan

Develop a communication plan to serve four purposes:

- Align on goals and objectives
- Provide project updates with reciprocating feedback and recognition
- Convey any resource needs such as staff, technology, or training
- Collaborate on your career development needs

It is easier to have these kinds of critical discussions when time is already allocated on both of your schedules rather than having to find each other for impromptu conversations. Talk to your manager about these topics and ask how she would best like to stay connected. Suggest three aspects for your joint communication plan:

1. **Schedule routine meetings every two weeks.** Share an agenda that may include updating projects and objectives, discussing career development plans, and requesting needed resources. The topics and duration will vary each meeting, but this ensures you will have a forum to touch base regularly.

2. **Send a brief note each Friday with project status.** You may consider highlighting major accomplishments in green, items that need further discussion in red, and tasks that are progressing on plan in yellow. This will help you stay aligned and support recognition and feedback as well.

3. **Plan an informal quarterly breakfast or lunch.** The intent is to build rapport through casual discussion about how things

are going and what's on each other's mind. Certainly, you may choose to prepare your topics and questions in advance to ensure your objectives are met.

Your manager may be less structured than you are, in which case they may opt not to schedule these items in advance but keep them on your action list so you can propose these forums in a seemingly less structured way.

## Managing Misalignment

Creating a purposeful bond from the start takes a lot of time and effort. However, it is much easier to maintain the positive relationship going forward than to fix a dysfunctional relationship later, often when operational issues arise, emotions are high, and patience runs thin. Misalignment with managers is the most common form of frustration for employees. Introverts may be tempted to absorb all the blame or write off the connection entirely. However, moments of reflection and communication may help preserve the relationship and potentially be a catalyst for enhanced rapport going forward.

Certainly, if you are being harassed or subject to inappropriate behavior from your manager or anyone else at work, this is never acceptable, and you have the responsibility to yourself and to the company to bring these issues to the appropriate authority immediately.

Otherwise, if you sense that the relationship is deteriorating, employ this six-step **REPAIR** model:

1. **Review the situation:** Take time alone and jot down the issues. What is not going well? Are you two not talking or misaligned? Are you not getting the support you need? Are you getting "too much" support? Also, be honest in assessing your own

contributions to the problem at hand. Are you sharing? Are you involving your manager as needed? Do you feel the job or expectations have changed? Note what is still going well. What do you still enjoy from the job and relationship with your manager? Write it all down. Don't filter your thoughts. You won't be sharing this piece of paper, but it helps to get all your concerns out of your head.

2. **Explore the root cause:** Once you have flushed out your thoughts and concerns, review them. Ask yourself "why" when evaluating each source of concern. Then seek the common thread throughout your list. Usually there is one root cause. You can test out your candidates by asking yourself if this one facet of the relationship improved, would it fix most or all of the issues you wrote down in the first step?

3. **Prospect for solutions:** Based on the root cause you have identified, put together a list of ideas that could help. This might include a discussion of your goals and expectations or a heart-to-heart talk with your manager.

4. **Ask for other opinions:** Talk to a detached confidante: your spouse, a friend, a mentor, a sponsor, or a Human Resources representative. Just be sure you are comfortable with this person and they understand the need for confidentiality. This step is critical to ensure you are evaluating the situation fairly and without emotion, and that your approach to improving the situation is practical.

5. **Initiate a discussion with your manager:** After reviewing the situation and possible solutions, you may decide you don't need a discussion with your manager. However, remember that you raised this issue to yourself because of apprehensions or frustrations. Nervousness about having a conversation is not a good reason to shelve the talk. If it is truly an issue, it

will likely fester until it becomes a bigger problem. Instead, practice how you might open the discussion. You do not need to make a formal declaration. You may just open by asking your manager how she thinks things are going. Are there ways the two of you can raise the team's performance by improving communication or alignment? This often invites open dialogue, during which you can mention your concerns in a constructive manner. Be sure not to make unilateral charges but instead offer positive steps you may take and invite your manager's ideas. If the conversation doesn't appear to be addressing the root cause or solutions you developed, raise them directly so you can make real progress. Nearly all issues can be resolved or at least managed with communication if one person suggests a discussion and shares the willingness to talk. The biggest problems arise when neither party takes the initiative, in which case considerable grief usually lies ahead.

6. **Raise the issue to others**: If a situation does become unbearable and direct communication has failed to improve the situation, don't just let it lie. Schedule a private meeting with your Human Resources representative to discuss the issue. If there are irreconcilable differences, they may offer to mediate or propose other solutions.

## Despair Without REPAIR

After several years in an assignment, I was offered an exciting new position just as my manager departed. However, his replacement asked me to stay to lead a reorganization and a fresh approach. My sense of loyalty to the team and the ego boost of feeling indispensable led me to stay, foregoing the other opportunity. In hindsight, I did not think this decision through thoroughly.

Within a couple of months, it was clear my values and styles were quite different from my new manager's. She was rather harsh, disrespectful of the group's expertise, and determined to push her change agenda without much consultation. My own pride and stubborn refusal to relent, paired with her ego and determination, meant we never had a meeting to put all these issues on the table and seek a path forward. Instead, the issues continued to grow until it became unbearable for both of us. Only four months after joining her team, I was relegated to projects until I landed my next assignment elsewhere in the company.

Several years later, as I prepared to retire, I arranged an amicable lunch with my former manager. Without the pressure of an employer-employee relationship, we both shared our frustrations. We quickly concluded that we both had good points and that we should have met for a discussion years ago. Perhaps such communication would have dispelled assumptions and conclusions we had both built up in our heads and enabled us to work together in a more productive manner. However, neither of us had worked the process described here. We both endured many days and nights of frustration that might have been avoided.

Your relationship with your manager will always be the most important bond at work. As such, nurture it every day. Employ the REPAIR model before any issues become insurmountable. Your own challenges, successes, and tactics with each of your managers serve as perfect training ground for the leader you wish to be.

## Healthy Environment

Just as your tree needs to have healthy roots nourished by water and minerals, it also needs the right environment with ample sunlight. Every tree thrives in certain climates and struggles in others. You need to find the right environment for you. If your best efforts still leave you unsatisfied, it may not be the right fit for you, in which case it is time to change environments so you can flourish.

## ACTIONS:

1. Would you consider the rapport with your manager to be strong? Why or why not?

2. Do you have enough touch points with your manager?

3. Have you shared your introversion as a building block for greater communication and productivity?

4. Do you feel you have the appropriate level of communication with your manager to drive alignment, feedback, and recognition? If not, consider how you may broach the issue to improve the interaction.

5. If you are misaligned with your manager, initiate the REPAIR model to try to patch up the situation and move forward together.

***The Corporate Introvert*** **– Accompanying Worksheets**

Free Worksheets accompany most chapters so you can record your strengths, values, and passions and develop your own plan to apply your talents to become a confident and authentic leader.

https://www.BeyondIntroversion.com/tci-landing-page

Chapter Eleven

# CREATING THE RIGHT FIT

*"Everyone shines, given the right lighting."*
*–Susan Cain, introvert revolutionary and author of Quiet (1968- )*

Have you ever been driving along daydreaming and suddenly wonder how you got to where you are? It's quite scary. You were on automatic pilot, consumed by your busy day and now you may find yourself in a place you don't want to be.

Our careers can be that way at times. We pause and in a moment of clarity we wonder, "How did I get here?" Perhaps you are happy with your good fortune, or maybe you wish you had paid more attention and thought through a plan.

You can avoid much of the frustrations of a job that doesn't fit your personality or a career that doesn't meet your lifestyle plans simply by tapping a common introvert strength—planning—to consider options along your career path. Most job mismatches occur when people don't assess their own strengths and passions or uncover the choices that lay all around them. They start their job search process by scattering résumés in many directions, often prepared to take the first job offer or decide amongst options based largely on salary. There is little consideration for finding the right "fit" to meet your strengths, ambitions, and lifestyle plans.

This chapter focuses on roles that may meet your interests, rather than specific jobs or titles. We will wrap up with the REACH model to provide structure during job transitions throughout your career.

## Five Fundamental Roles That Make a Difference

Every company performs five activities to meet their owners' or shareholders' objectives and deliver goods and services profitably. Each job within the company contributes to one or more of these activities. Which fundamental role(s) are you currently engaged in? Do you find the objectives and tasks motivating and rewarding? Do they fit with most of your strengths and passions?

### 1. Money Maker

Every company must ring the cash register. They sell something, whether a product or service. Roles that monetize these products or services are at the heart of every company. They may come in the form of salespeople, traders, program marketers, or customer service representatives. People in these roles typically have strong interpersonal skills. They need to build relationships internally and with prospective clients. They should understand the value of the product, the needs of their customers, and how they can match those two perspectives to create revenue.

## 2. Cost Saver

Given that profit margin is the difference between sales price and the cost of goods, minimizing the costs of raw materials, distribution, facilities, and equipment generates greater profit. Otherwise, you can lose money regardless of the level of sales. People in cost-reduction roles understand how things are made, moved, and sold. They evaluate process design and try to drive productivity throughout the system, both through efficient use of manpower as well as machinery and time. These people are often keen observers, thrive on analysis, and are 24/7 problem solvers.

## 3. Creative Innovator

Every business seeks to differentiate itself by offering unique products and services. They strive to create products that consumers find valuable. The world is constantly changing. Companies that are able to innovate and adjust rapidly to changes in the world around them have the opportunity to thrive. Otherwise, they will eventually be left behind. Whether they call it research and development (R&D), product design, or entrepreneurship, businesses want to hire the brightest, most creative minds to improve current products and find the next invention to give them a leg up.

## 4. Functional Expert

Every company needs technical expertise in a variety of areas. Oil companies need engineers to drill for oil or run chemical plants. Silicon Valley companies need computer techies to program and create. Most companies also need expertise and guidance from legal, accounting, and human resource staff to ensure adherence to rules and standards. Each of these functional areas is charged with performing a particular task and doing it well. Each has its own skillset, but at its core, they are subject matter experts. These roles involve less guessing and risk taking and more deep knowledge and efficiency to use their skills to successfully complete tasks and guide others.

5. **Leader**

Organizations need every role—sales, process management, R&D, and functional expertise—to perform well if they are to generate profit margin. Each group needs leadership to oil the gears, so their teams work smoothly. More importantly, all these functions must work well together, supporting each other toward achievement of a common goal. We will cover team leadership in considerable detail in Section IV.

## Introvert Roles

You might be curious about which of the five fundamental roles are "made for introverts" and which are not. Many assume customer-interfacing roles (Money Maker) are far more comfortable for extroverts. Those same people often assume that more in-depth, stable roles of Functional Experts are conducive to most introverts' skillsets. These assumptions are understandable, but flawed.

As revealed in the Introvert Talent Quiz, everyone is different. While most respondents tended to prefer structured, detailed roles, many have considerable creative, leadership, and social skills. Recall the Energy Equation, as our working definition of introversion, does not discount an introvert's ability to succeed in any of these roles. In fact, many introverts are uniquely qualified; they just need time to reenergize during the day to deliver consistently.

Introverts are particularly valuable in high-ticket, long-term, complex sales. Their distinctive skills soar in understanding customer needs, convincing people of value, influencing behavioral change, and implementing original products or services. According to Alicia Dale, successful salesperson at Ryder Transportation and GE Capital, some of the best salespeople are introverts who use their strengths of deep product knowledge and personal, authentic relationships with key stakeholders as their means to drive sales.[16] Many introverts are poised to help fill the leadership gaps of today and tomorrow with a thoughtful, loyal, balanced approach. So, there truly is no right or wrong answer here. The key is to honestly explore and embrace your strengths and seek roles that tap those skills you enjoy most.

## Are You a Generalist or a Specialist?

Some people want to be specialists, developing deep expertise, often in a narrow range of tasks, products, or teams. Others prefer to be generalists, leaning on subject matter experts while they coordinate and drive initiatives across a variety of jobs during their career. Companies need those with deep knowledge to innovate, problem solve, and carry the history of the organization, as well as those who help coordinate and share best practices across business units.

This distinction is worth exploring because each taps a different set of skills and styles. Over time you will find which career path fits you best. Rather early in my career I realized I was a generalist. I loved learning aspects of different roles and departments. By moving to different jobs every few years, I avoided the boredom I feared and quenched my curiosity. I also realized such a transitory career meant that networking would be critical, and I would frequently be striking up new relationships with managers, team members, and key stakeholders. I discovered those would be challenging aspects for a generalist, but it fit my passions and thus my career path.

## The Drive to Job Search

In a long career, you may search for your next job about ten times—whether it's at the next desk over, or at a completely different company or industry. Maybe you will have a chance to form your own company. Introverts who resist the pressure to network and fear the unknown may prefer to stay put. However, there are several reasons to stretch your comfort zone and grow through job transition.

## Upgrade

You've been in a job for a while. Initially, you climbed a steep learning curve to become a significant contributor. Now, you have checked all your career planning boxes regarding what you want to get out of the assignment. Sure, you love the job, the people, and the comfort you have every day, so it's easy to stay for a while longer and enjoy the fruits of your labor. However, Michelle Lax, retired senior manager at the largest producer of construction aggregate in the US, asserts: "The longer you continue to stay in a role, you are not adding to your résumé." You risk getting pigeonholed, and it will become hard to restart your career. If your personal target is contentment, you may choose to stay. However, if you aim to flourish, it is time to move on. There are plenty of opportunities out there that value and need your expertise. Time to dust off your résumé!

## Refit

This job and company or team appeared to be a good match when you joined. Perhaps it was a fine fit for months or years, but things have changed for you. Your skills, values, or interests may have shifted and the job is now boring and your passion is fading. Possibly the company, management strategy, or job expectations have evolved and now you are charged to perform tasks you don't enjoy. You may choose to be open-minded and consider how you may stretch and grow in an evolving definition of your job, but it may also be a sign it's time to seek the next role. Sara Bonario reflects: "I think many people wake up... in their late 40s or early 50s and have their mid-life crisis, which may include realizing they can no longer accept working for a company [or job] that... doesn't give them personal satisfaction."

## Unmanageable Relationships

We discussed how to cultivate a symbiotic relationship with your manager in the last chapter. Suffice to say that disagreements with your manager may fester to the point where a change is necessary. Our values and interests evolve, and minor differences may become annoying over time. Acknowledging differences and agreeing on creative ways of working together can solve many disagreements and be a tangible personal growth experience. However, such efforts take two and are best tackled early on. If this isn't possible, you both may agree a change is necessary.

## Forced Downsizing

Sometimes a job change is not within your control. This happens to the best of people and workers. Companies downsize due to financial challenges or management changes. Teams shrink, groups combine, businesses get sold off. It's easy to bemoan your misfortunes or vilify those who put you on the chopping block, but it is wasted energy that you should be using to regroup and find that next role. Embrace the change as the opportunity it can be—perhaps this is the best thing for you and your career.

## Narrow Your Interests to the Best Job Prospects: REACH for the Stars

Once you decide to change jobs, you may be tempted to expedite the process and rapidly secure a job to end the torment. Stop! Take the time to put yourself in the best position to reach for your next great job. What makes a job great? It's rarely salary or title. Boston Consulting Group's Decoding Global Talent report of 200,000 survey responses found salary was the eighth ranked factor for employee happiness. The number one factor was "appreciation for your work," with other top considerations including work-life balance, learning and career development, and relationships with colleagues and superiors.[17] Get prepared first through the **REACH** Model:

- **Review** your roots (strengths, values, mindsets, and ambitions). Remind yourself of these items in advance so you are driven toward the right fit, not by the emotions of the search itself.

- **Evaluate** the tasks you enjoy the most. What activities at work or at home light your passion? Once you think of jobs in this way, your job options expand considerably. You may like details and numbers. Those leanings fit well in your current accountancy role, but you don't have to limit yourself to another accounting position. Don't define yourself as "Mary the Accountant", but perhaps as "Mary the curious, driven, analytic." Many jobs use these same skills such as finance, comptroller, auditing, and business analysis—both in your current company and across other

146

industries. Remain open-minded, creative, and persistent in broadening your search. Gather ideas and suggestions from mentors, role models, sponsors, managers, and human resources. Every job search benefits from a wide scope.

- **Assess** your wish list. There is no perfect job, but putting together a list of "must-haves" and "nice-to-haves" early in the process avoids wasting time and provides a framework for your research before and during interviews, as well as for evaluating job offers later. Items you may consider for your lists could include key tasks, team chemistry, level of autonomy, work/life balance including travel and after-hours expectations, work environment including closed-door offices or cubicles, office location, commute, company and team culture, and pay and benefits. Definitely aim high, but also maintain a sense of flexibility.

- **Cultivate** your network. Certainly, personal connections with the posting manager or any external sites will greatly improve your candidacy. Introverts may have a smaller network than others, but the quality of your connections and your determination make the difference. Build your list of connections within these three groups:

  - Personal relationships: family, friends, college classmates, church members
  - Work colleagues: co-workers, internal or external customers, past managers, HR
  - Job search experts: college career placement officers, headhunters

- Reference the material in Chapter 9 to discover how to apply your personal strengths to create a strong network.

- **Hunt** for information on your prospects. Check out websites of the industries you are interested in and the companies you are considering. These are great resources to understand the five fundamental roles we discussed earlier in this chapter. Study prospective companies and seek answers to the Revealing Questions below.

---

### Revealing Questions

o   What are their recruiting objectives and tactics?

o   What are their benefits, work locations, and culture?

o   What are their values? How do they treat their employees?

o   What are their views on diversity and is that reflected in their statistics?

o   What is the work/life balance? Can you expect to work nights and weekends often?

o   How is corporate culture defined or represented in material?

o   Is the environment more competitive or collaborative?

o   How are staff developed and recognized?

o   Can you see yourself in the pictures on their website?

o   Does your intuition say this will fit well, or do you have a nagging concern?

---

Besides studying companies, research posting managers on corporate websites and through social media. Where are they in the corporate structure? What is their role? What is their background?

All these will provide insight, quench your curiosity, and help you feel more at ease in an upcoming interview.

Your research won't answer all your questions, but it should give you a sense of overall fit and help you decide if you want to pursue a job further. By working the steps in the **REACH** model, you should generate a list of prospects that you believe offers exciting potential matches.

The job search process is often a rollercoaster of hopes, dreams, missed opportunities, crushed expectations, and glorious success. It can be especially exhausting for introverts, in part because we seemingly have little control over the outcome and because our communications and networking skills are put to the test. However, like most tasks, introverts benefit from a different approach.

Remind yourself of your roots. Focus on what you can control. Practice self-compassion and lean on your strengths. Preparation will help break down the process into manageable steps and curious learning will guide you to gather the necessary information to make the best decisions. Finally, resiliency will enable you to weather the inevitable emotional ride of anxiety and elation.

Some people are quite frustrated with their job while others don't feel fulfilled. Many endure this displeasure for fear of putting themselves out there through an arduous application process. The answer is not to endure, but to thoroughly prepare and reach for your dreams.

## Transitioning Roles

It doesn't matter if you are changing companies, teams, or chairs in the same group, the excitement of a new job quickly gives way to the apprehension of the challenges and opportunities ahead. It's an exciting time to assess your own approach and to focus on your priorities.

## Lean on Your Learning

Temper your hesitations in order to get off on the right foot. If you managed the job search process well, your skills and passions should be aligned with your new job. This is also a great time to reflect on your last job. What did you like about it and what did you not enjoy? What did you like about yourself in your role and what did you want to improve? Do you want to be more vulnerable and personable with co-workers? Develop stronger rapport with your manager? Strike a better work/life balance? Did you feel disorganized? Were you true to yourself? This job change, no matter how subtle or dramatic, presents the chance for you to grow. These adjustments can make a big difference in your job satisfaction and overall happiness.

## Build Relationships First

You may prefer to roll up your sleeves and dive into learning the details and tasks of any job. This calms natural fears, and you can do much of this studying in blissful silence and solitude. However, as we examined in the previous chapter, I urge you to turn the tables and begin with relationships first. Most introverts can struggle with casual acquaintances. Rather than avoiding them altogether, invest time toward building the deeper relations you may crave as an introvert. This process may generate plenty of discomfort, but you are establishing important rapport and removing other's misperceptions of introverts in the workplace. It may seem like the soft stuff, but relationship work is the glue that holds you, the job, and the team together.

## Finding the Fit

Ensuring you create and nurture the right environment is critical to the health and vibrancy of your tree. You should be driven by goals you have a passion for and determined to achieve your objectives your way. If your strengths and passions align with the company culture and specific role, your trunk will be stronger and your branches will expand toward the sky.

## ACTIONS:

1. Review your roots (strengths, values, mindsets, and ambitions).

2. Which of the fundamental role(s) are you most interested in? Is that aligned with your current role or ambitions?

3. In applying for jobs, think broadly about targeted tasks and culture, not titles.

4. When the opportunity for a job change does occur, step back and calmly assess the situation and how you can apply your strengths and the REACH model to make this a positive step.

## The Introvert Leadership Quiz

Discover how well you are employing your own strengths at work. You will receive an instant score and information about how to apply your strengths in traditionally challenging work situations.

https://forms.gle/d9h1n4jPeS3NRTyK8

## Section IV:

# BLOSSOMING LEADER

Nurtured in the right environment, our canopy becomes strong and beautiful. Just as our tree blossoms and later sheds its seedlings across the field, we too have the opportunity to impart our knowledge across the organization.

Some people do not consider introverts to be natural leaders. Yet we know that employees often seek the exact attributes that define introverts: good listeners, kind confidantes, curious learners, resilient problem solvers, and determined leaders. Many introverts are perfectly suited to lead teams large and small. However, many are unsure if they are prepared or willing to make the leap to leadership.

Section IV focuses on why your organization needs you, why you are well suited to lead teams, and how you can make an impact as a supervisor by applying your unique perspective to team forming and employee development. As a leader, suddenly you become responsible not only for your own tasks and projects, but also for selecting, developing, and promoting each individual in your group and most especially the interwoven community of your overall team. This can be a daunting opportunity for anyone. The key is to trust your authentic self to succeed. In this last section, we will cover four critical aspects of your leadership role:

1. **Role Model:** filling the role as the leader of teams

2. **Team Builder**: how to form teams that are cohesive and successful

3. **Culture Creator**: how to build a team's brand

4. **Team Coach**: how to support teams and conduct difficult conversations

Each aspect contributes to the successful leadership of an accomplished team.

This leadership section begins with a discussion about the Leadership Gap. Conditions are ripe for introverts to fill this gap. It's your chance to make a difference for your team and organization. Your tree is strong. Many will rely upon your power and wisdom to help them succeed and become the next generation of leaders. Now you are ready to use your superpowers to guide others. Do you hear the call?

Chapter Twelve

# THE GAP NEEDS YOU

*"Why not see what happens when you challenge your employees to bring all of their talents to their job and reward them not for doing it just like everyone else, but for pushing the envelope, being adventurous, creative, and open-minded, and trying new things?"*
*–Tony Hsieh, American internet entrepreneur and former CEO of Zappos (1973-2020)*

What is a leadership gap and why does it matter to you? Companies are looking at the required number and competencies of leaders they need now and into the future and they're concerned. Seventy-seven percent of companies identified a leadership gap in 2019.[18] The chasm relates to both quantity and quality. According to Forbes, only 14% of CEOs have the leadership talent they need to grow their businesses.[19]

Let's look at how this leadership gap can empower introverts and reshape your career.

## Quantity: Shortfall of Leaders

Let's first focus on the thinning pipeline of corporate leaders. Every day 10,000 Baby Boomers are retiring![20] Many of these are corporate leaders. Meanwhile, disgruntled Gen X staff that form the backbone of rising leadership are leaving for the more flexible gig economy and the more personable small business community. Finally, Gen Y/Millennials, the natural managerial successors over the next decade, are much less patient to wait for leadership positions. More than four out of five Millennials will stay in their jobs for three years or less.[21] These generations are not tied to companies and the golden parachutes of pensions and retirement funds like veteran workers. All have good reason to look elsewhere. Loyalty has plummeted as corporate restructuring has increased the cycle of consolidations and layoffs. Thus, the corporate leadership gap grows.

Yet large companies continue to fuel the economy and employ over half[22] of the US workforce. Companies are recognizing the gap and challenges ahead, though they are admittedly late in addressing this changing dynamic.

So, what is the solution? Companies need to broaden their search for leaders and implement programs that develop people to lead in the decades ahead. Many plan to meet this leadership gap by tapping a diverse set of employees, including minorities and women.[23]

Today, most leaders are white males. In fact, a survey of S&P 500 companies in 2019 revealed female CEOs were outnumbered by CEOs named James 27 to 24![24] This sounds comical, but it underscores the severe lack of diversity in senior leadership positions, and it flows to all levels throughout companies. Minorities are also underrepresented. Despite accounting for 12% of the US population, African Americans fill only 3.2% of senior leadership roles according to a CBS News study in 2019.[25]

Do you know who else is underrepresented? Although introverts account for approximately 50% of the general population and corporate workforce, according to an Industrial Psychology study, only two percent of senior leaders claim to be introverts. Two percent![26] This may be understated, as many people tend to hide their introversion. However, even if the true number is ten times higher (20%). introverts are still severely underrepresented in leadership positions. These metrics don't improve much elsewhere amongst the leadership ranks. Only seven percent of front-line managers claim to be introverted.[27]

## Quality: Skillset Gap

A lack of quality or skills further contributes to the leadership gap. Consultants believe key business indicators of the late twentieth century—driving strategy, delivering financial results, managing operations well—are now complemented by twenty-first century needs for transparency and overcoming ambiguity.[28] The business world is increasingly complex and skeptical.

- Companies are trying to decipher changing consumer demands in an increasingly competitive environment.
- Consumers want to trust companies they do business with and appreciate those who care to invest in community and environment.

- Meanwhile, employees are seeking an unprecedented level of clarity and balance in their work life, as well as reciprocating loyalty and respect from their employer.

STRATX[29], an innovative global management development and consulting firm, highlights four essential talents for future business success:

1. **Critical Thinking**: Balanced analysis matched with decision making skills.

2. **Curiosity and Innovation**: Open-mindedness and observation of changing environments in order to discover products and processes.

3. **Emotional Intelligence**: A resilient mindset supporting collaboration, teamwork, and leadership to drive diverse perspectives and thinking.

4. **Technological Savvy**: Observing and creating step changes in technological capability.

It's no coincidence that common introvert strengths align favorably with STRATX's four critical talents for future business. In fact, recent neurological research indicates introverts have thicker gray matter in their pre-frontal cortex, often considered the origin for executive functions such as planning, decision making, abstract thought, resilience, and self-control. (An extrovert's thinner gray matter suggests they are less cerebral in lieu of more seat-of-the-pants decision making.[30])

Introverts tend to be strong leaders for independent, proactive teams who appreciate a supportive, calm, collaborative style.[31] The command-and-control style of many extroverts may work well with passive followers seeking guidance, but this is quickly becoming the workforce of the past.

# Filling the Gap

We have established that introverts are poised to help fill leadership vacancies and bring a style that fits well with team needs in the twenty-first century. Just look at the quotes at the beginning of each of our chapters. All of them are from self-professed introverts. Most are leaders in their field of business, the arts, or sports. When introverts lean on their strengths, we can quite capably bust myths and manage social situations, conduct productive meetings, and make strong decisions. Introverts have robust innate tendencies and, even more, the ambition to contribute and lead.

Ultimately, companies need a diverse workforce of women and men, people of every color and nationality, introverts and extroverts. After all, this combination represents society's demographics and thus helps build a distinct connection with the needs of the consumers that businesses aim to serve. Furthermore, this community brings an assortment of perspectives, ideas, and styles that aid companies in tackling problems and charting unique paths. Clearly, today's underrepresented women, minorities, and introverts are needed to fill both the sheer number and the skillset gaps already persistent in corporate leadership.

# Where Are the Introverts?

So why are introverts so underrepresented in corporate leadership? First, we should consider that many companies are still greatly affected by societal norms that assume that leaders should look formidable, speak loudly, and make rapid decisions. Thus, they place extroverts into the vast majority of leadership positions. Most people see strength in employees like themselves, and extroverts are no different. They tend to promote extroverts, and don't provide opportunities to the quieter staff on their team.

Yes, stereotypes need to change, and companies need to promote more diversity through structured leadership programs, but the responsibility also lies with each of us, the introverts of the corporate world. We need to shift our own belief that introversion is a burden, or that we are second-rate to extroverts. We need to identify our strengths and finally recognize that these skills are now the key to both corporate success and our own dreams. Embrace these strengths. Learn about them and practice them so they are indeed your superpowers.

Rather early in my career, I was overcome by the preponderance of loudness, ego, and spontaneous debate around me. I tried to compete but shrunk under the realization this was not my style. This was neither comforting to myself nor effective for my team. Yet my fear of failure and my personal need to live up to my own lofty standards put me under tremendous pressure. I tried my best to cope and appeared to have it all together, but away from the eyes of managers and co-workers, I crumbled. I put on weight, drank too much at corporate social events, and picked up rashes and nervous disorders that hinted at the trouble inside.

When I reached my breaking point mid-career, I fought the inclination to either persist or leave my company, instead opting to shift my approach, to find a more authentic style. It appears a lot easier to go with the flow, but it takes courage to chart your own path. I began to rely on my strengths of personal connection and preparation to consider and include others' perspectives. That simple shift changed my career. I began to discover my own style based on my strengths and comfort zones. My self-confidence recovered and my teams began to over deliver. I was finally at peace with myself.

## Are You Ready to Lead?

We've now identified the solution to the leadership gap. Yet many introverts aren't convinced they actually want to fill that gap. Why not?

Many experienced employees don't show an interest in leadership because the job just doesn't sound appealing. Newer staff may confuse *leadership* with *management* and fear it is fraught with paperwork and metrics. Others don't feel they are natural leaders and don't find their companies' training programs (if they exist at all) to be effective. Companies certainly need to address these issues, but for employees reading this book, you should be armed with information.

In the next chapter we will review seven key roles that managers need to fill to lead their teams to individual and group success. The call to action is clear; you need to decide if you want to answer that call. You can be a big part of the solution to the growing leadership gap!

## ACTIONS:

1. How would you assess the leadership gap at your current company? Does the company recognize that gap?

2. Learn more about leadership in your organization so you can determine your own career path.

3. Does your company actively identify and recruit diverse leadership candidates both within and outside the company?

4. Does your company offer a leadership development program that includes mentorships, role models, and leadership experiences throughout your career? Do you participate in such programs?

Chapter Thirteen

# THE LEADERSHIP
# ROLE MODEL

*"A good leader inspires people to have confidence in the leader.*
*A great leader inspires people to have confidence in themselves."*
*−Eleanor Roosevelt, American diplomat and activist (1884-1962)*

People may avoid leadership opportunities or come up short in fulfilling such jobs because they aren't truly informed about what the role entails. Whether you have been frustrated as a supervisor trying to lead like everyone else or you aspire to lead, this chapter will help you consider the responsibilities of leadership and how you can perform the various roles using your own approach.

## Is Leadership Right for You?

All leadership roles are not alike, so consider the factors covered in Chapter 11, Creating The Right Fit. You may be happy to find challenge and contribution as a leader inside your team or you may opt for a more formal supervisory position when the right opportunity develops. Every organization needs both types of leadership. As you influence others within your work team you can decide what form of leadership is right for you.

Team leadership often requires stretching your comfort zone, so you must judge for yourself if the benefits are worthwhile. Supervisory roles carry the tremendous responsibilities of team selection and employee coaching and motivation, as well as the necessities of conflict resolution and administrative duties. Many will prefer to avoid these extra responsibilities. For the uninformed introvert, these tasks may appear overwhelming.

However, with talent and mindset as your roots, leadership may become a career ambition, a natural direction for your growth. Leading is a great way to quench your passion to help others and make a difference in your business, while cultivating the leaders of tomorrow. Succeeding in these areas can be the highlight of your day and career.

Not surprisingly, the best way to be a great leader is to do it your way. With courage and determination, you can dispel myths and tackle the challenges that each branch of your tree represents by leaning on your authentic talents. To lead any other way is self-destructive.

If you dedicate yourself to such an approach, being a supervisor is the most rewarding aspect of work. Once I discovered a style that was consistent with my personal strengths, my greatest thrill was seeing team members grow, gain confidence, and contribute their talents to the organization. This joy makes the journey worthwhile for each leader.

# Being a Role Model

Leadership is not simple. You will play several roles every day, going well beyond the hiring, firing, and coaching challenges discussed in subsequent chapters. By the nature of your title, you are a role model. Your team is watching you—your work ethic, your behavior, your priorities. In order to earn their respect, you first need to be aware of the various roles you occupy.

However, before you roll up your sleeves and approach the leadership responsibilities merely as a task list, remember that passion, energy, and dedication go a long way in earning respect. Perception is reality. People may observe you and take away an impression far from what you intended. Many tend to mistake an introvert's focus and determination for self-absorption and aloofness. Once they apply these labels, it can be difficult to replace them. You spent the first section of this book discovering your strengths, values, and mindsets. As a manager, depend on your self-awareness and passions to demonstrate a more endearing and inspiring approach. This provides a solid base for being a role model to your team.

# Leadership Roles

You have seven primary roles as a leader: strong link, reliable guide, rules champion, bridge builder, composed rock, team advocate, and helicopter pilot. Each is an important function for you to embody. These roles apply to all leaders, regardless of their personality type, but introverts will find it best to utilize common strengths such as thoughtfulness, resiliency, and loyalty to establish a leadership foundation.

The skills for each of these roles develop over time. Management should not expect leaders to be ready-made for these responsibilities. Certain skills may seem to come naturally, while others take focused work. That is okay. We are all different, and the best companies recognize their organization is made from a broad spectrum of leadership skills and styles meshed together.

## Strong Link

Picture your team as a chain. The best teams are made of strong links across the chain. Everyone contributes and relies upon each other. A weak link can break the chain. You are part of that chain. You, too, need to be a strong link.

Every manager has their own job tasks, such as strategic thinking and managing stakeholders, in addition to leading the team. You are the only one that can do these tasks. Many managers get so wrapped up in micro-managing each team member that they ignore their own responsibilities. By doing so you are not only frustrating your staff, but you are also neglecting your own duties. Don't become a weak link in your own team's chain.

At the beginning of her career, Jay Artale used to go into meetings and try to effect change but found it akin to cold calling and couldn't get anyone to commit. Then she saw how her boss's manager operated. When he had a concept, he would spend weeks before a critical meeting selling his idea to all the key stakeholders who could get in his way or help him achieve success. As a result, the meeting to effect change became merely a final seal of approval. This stakeholder management was a key role that was critical to the team's success. This manager was fulfilling his role as a strong link, and he also served as a role model in Jay's development.

## Reliable Guide

As a leader, you should be a reliable guide, trusted and accessible as well as transparent and giving of your time and knowledge. Maintain an open-door policy to your staff not only by being available, but truly listening, taking action, and maintaining confidences. Staff don't need to see or talk to you every day, but they want to be confident that they can rely on you when they need to. Provide insights into often mysterious corporate processes like annual evaluations, promotion considerations, and career planning. I'm not advocating disclosing corporate secrets, but sharing how these processes work reduces the apprehension in these areas and creates a sense of openness and confidence in your leadership style.

Matt Kingsolver notes that he "find(s) the open door is not always just about time, but about content. That is, it's important that your team feels it can be open and honest with you without unfair repercussions, that you listen and take action on their ideas."

This sharing of time and insights extends beyond your team. Forty-five percent of respondents to our Introvert Talent Quiz indicated they were mentoring at least one other employee. Be a mentor to others, including newer members of the organization. Form a mentoring circle for introverts. Find ways to share your experience and create a more open environment in your organization. You will benefit as much as others do. Such engagements help you to keep a pulse on a wide array of generational styles and diverse viewpoints, so you don't get stuck in your ways.

## Rules Champion

All employees are expected to follow company rules. As a leader and role model, you need to be aware of all the rules and adhere to them every day. This seems obvious and simple, but you probably have a myriad of requirements that are often shared through a thick PowerPoint slide pack or lengthy orientation meeting on day one and filed thereafter. You are responsible for knowing the rules and training and implementing these expectations for the whole team. Include expert resources such as corporate human resources, ethics and compliance officers, and legal counsel as needed to decipher unclear circumstances.

Sara Bonario shares: "Passionate people with a strong set of core values in my opinion will demonstrate these traits... It is just how they show up in the world." Following these rules is part of the organization's license to operate, and it is the leader's role to ensure compliance.

## Bridge Builder

Another role is to act as the bridge between your team and others, including senior leadership, other intra-company organizations, and external partners and competitors. While your team members will develop working relationships with groups and counterparties, you should be aligned with them in building similar relations with your equals in the same organizations. This will require building rapport, mining for information, advocating for your team members, and solving problems that might arise between organizations. These social and occasionally contentious situations can appear daunting to many introverts. Use your strengths to prepare for discussions, customize your engagements through less formal, small encounters, and pair up with a team member or others to diffuse social pressures, especially with initial interactions.

Michelle Lax, retired senior manager, shares that a key priority for her was to "build relationships with all [her] key co-workers. This helps get things done more effectively. It can also help you if you do have any issues with your manager or if you are looking for a change. Keep up with these connections." Building this rapport in advance will pay dividends when called upon.

You will also be expected to rise above company silos and narrow objectives to do the right thing for the overall corporation. This can be a tricky role to balance within your tight-knit team, but you are modeling proper priorities. Lead by example to work closely within your manager's team and with other company leaders to explore synergies, knock down barriers, and share best practices.

## Composed Rock

To be composed is to be calm under pressure and manage your emotions with purpose. Your team and others are watching when the heat is turned up, when there is a safety issue or a security breach, when a team member starts yelling, or when someone cries under personal or work pressures. I've seen all these emotions at work. To be clear, I don't suggest being cold and emotionless. Rather, sort through the situation and respond empathetically. Crumbling under pressure does not evoke confidence from your team members. You may be sweating inside, but your ability to temper the situation, find the root cause, and solve the problem will solidify your leadership and provide an example for others to follow.

This requires mindfulness to consciously decide on your approach rather than getting caught up in the emotions of the moment. Make the effort to pause and evaluate options in your head. Eventually, through practice, this more tempered and purposeful method will become second nature. Especially in crisis, your reactions can build tremendous confidence and loyalty amongst the team, or they can raise doubt and dissent amongst members.

In my first weeks at the Detroit Distribution Terminal, the entire plant shut down in the middle of the night due to an operational issue. Though I was not the mechanic, I immediately headed to the plant to lend leadership to the situation. I managed changing schedules for our truck drivers, concerns from service station owners regarding delayed gasoline deliveries, and a mechanic who was frantic as he tried to repair the issue with all eyes seemingly on him. Though I was not an expert in these areas, my composure during this operational emergency helped get us back on track by the morning. The troops appreciated my leadership and willingness to roll up my sleeves alongside the team to navigate through a precarious situation.

## Team Advocate

As a team advocate, promote your team by creating opportunities for others to shine and then communicate their accomplishments to senior management. Everyone wants to feel appreciated. Spend time considering how to recognize staff with pats on the back, acknowledgement at meetings, personal thank-you notes, or gift cards. Certainly, when raises and promotions are justified, have your information ready to support such an assertion.

While it is always vital to share your team members' achievements, be careful not to embellish them, as this undermines their true accomplishments and may jeopardize your own credibility. Providing an accurate picture of your team's successes and development areas helps maintain the rapport, alignment, and trust you are striving for with your manager.

You may also advocate for your team by supporting their efforts to prioritize their time. Give them the authority to excuse themselves from superfluous meeting invitations or to minimize unnecessary training or other draws on their time.

The best way to advocate for your team is to engage and listen. Early in Todd Miner's career, he prioritized financial targets over team needs. He recalled: "My learning was that I did not elevate 'caring for others above the drive to deliver improvement." Later, he recognized his misstep and turned his early career shortcoming into a strength, advocating that for leaders, "truly caring for others' needs should be at the top of the list. This is an 'and' proposition. Caring for others *and* delivering performance."

Lean on your thoughtfulness trait. Simple acts of kindness and consideration go a long way. If you are not spending time each week on recognition, you should start today.

## Helicopter Pilot

A helicopter pilot can observe from a distance or land on the ground and get involved in the details. A leader must take both perspectives to satisfy the previous six roles along with the team building and coaching roles to follow. The key is determining when to observe and when to land. Everyone respects the manager who can lead the team's strategy and engage with senior leadership while also being comfortable to roll up their sleeves to help solve a problem that the team is tackling. However, no one likes a micro-manager or an absent leader. Neither is viewed as supportive or inspiring.

Leaders need to be a strong link in the team's chain, and they also need to work closely with team members to coach, motivate, and counsel. Artfully employing this balance will enable team members to benefit from the wisdom and inspiration you have to offer, while maintaining their own autonomy and style to deliver. To test if you are striking the right balance, have an open discussion with each of your staff about an appropriate level of involvement.

Certainly, there are times when you need to be more involved. Staff will need to be trained and indoctrinated into the team's culture and norms. Safety emergencies, operational crises, personal traumas will also benefit from your prompt attention and calm resiliency.

## Leadership is Within Your Grasp

The leadership gap needs you! You needn't relinquish your career plans to pursue leadership. You can still focus on your original ambitions while broadening your scope to lead and flourish.

As a team leader, you are tasked with many roles. Performing each role while balancing them with your team building and coaching responsibilities will always be a challenge. That's what makes leadership jobs hectic and turbulent but also so impactful, stimulating, and rewarding.

## ACTIONS:

1. Evaluate each team leader function. How do you think you are doing? Poll your team at your next meeting or anonymously through an online survey. Do they consider you a role model for each function? How can you improve?

    a. Strong Link

    b. Reliable Guide

    c. Rules Champion

    d. Bridge Builder

    e. Composed Rock

    f. Team Advocate

    g. Helicopter Pilot

### *The Corporate Introvert* – **Accompanying Worksheets**

Free Worksheets accompany most chapters so you can record your strengths, values, and passions and develop your own plan to apply your talents to become a confident and authentic leader.

https://www.BeyondIntroversion.com/tci-landing-page

## Chapter Fourteen

# TEAM SHAPING

*"A genuine leader is not a searcher for consensus but a molder of consensus."*
*—Dr. Martin Luther King, Jr., spokesperson and leader in the American Civil Rights movement (1929-1968)*

With the right people and atmosphere, teams can achieve amazing results, embodying the adage that the whole is greater than the sum of its parts. However, a dysfunctional team will quickly tumble and slowly drain your energy with infighting, misalignment, and repeated mistakes. You'll spend an inordinate amount of your time coaching staff, dealing with human resource issues, and managing high turnover. As an introvert, you've got the ideal traits for molding an exceptional team: thoughtfulness, listening, and loyalty. Build a foundation that sets the tone for the culture, coaching, and successes that are to follow.

# The SHAPE Team Building Model

What's the secret to building a successful team? After years gathering firsthand experience working for wise leaders and inept managers, along with my decades of learning and leading, I've summarized five essential factors in forming a team. Here are the guidelines to SHAPE your team:

1. **Skills Assessment**: Start by understanding what skills are necessary to achieve the team's mission and objectives. Do you need specific technical knowledge, creative innovators, organized project planners, or engaging customer service managers? Do you need experiences or connections with other organizations, outside companies, or industries? Once you identify all these necessary skills, list them down a column of a spreadsheet. Then list each of your team members, including yourself, in a row across the top. Check off which team members have the skills your team needs to succeed. No one, including the manager, will have them all. Once you have populated the spreadsheet, identify gaps or shortfalls.

2. **HR Planning**: Human Resource (HR) planning involves strategically forecasting the departure and arrival of employees. This succession plan is critical for smooth transitions and skills enrichment for every team. Use the same spreadsheet to note when you expect each of your staff members to move on. Naturally, a number of staff will be looking to contribute, gain experience, and move on to another challenge in short order. Others may be anxious to stay for several years to establish their expertise while others may be lifers, quite content to stay for the rest of their career. Also note those outside your team with particular skills who may prove to be qualified candidates to join your team in the future. When you overlay your team

member's plans with potential resources, you can begin to identify future skill gaps and possible solutions to cultivate.

3. **Aligning Culture:** You and your team must be fully aligned on your mission, vision, and values, which we will discuss in Chapter 15. Everyone should be focused and united on purpose and key deliverables. Without such effort, the team and certainly the individuals will wander, possibly dedicating tremendous effort tackling the wrong initiatives. Teams can overcome many challenges when they are motivated together.

4. **Perspectives:** Look for a diversity of perspectives, certainly including those of gender, age, or race. Your aim is to gather a variety of experiences and backgrounds on your team. You may want to include people who have started with your company straight out of college, others who come from a competitor or supplier, and others that have their MBA or served in the Armed Forces.

   By now you recognize the value of diversity of thought. Introverts will bring balanced analysis, creativity, empathy, and curiosity while extroverts will often contribute relationships, challenge, and quick thinking. These perspectives will foster creative approaches, innovative ways of thinking, imaginative problem-solving ideas, all of which can elevate teams from good to great. Diversity is not something to be forced upon you by corporate quotas. You should constantly seek a broad perspective to reap the competitive advantage it provides.

5. **Energy:** Each person contributes to building cohesive team chemistry. Everyone on the team needs to do more than just "get along." Exceptional teams support each other. They care for each other. They chip in where they can. They offer suggestions and tactful critique, and they accept the same without concern. Certain team members will naturally be more

confident, more ambitious in their career plans, and even more competitive than others. However, the sign of a great team is one in which each member, including the leader, puts aside their ego for the betterment of the team. A strongly connected team is focused, cares a lot, and laughs often.

## Team-First Approach

Team dynamics start at the top with you. If you truly believe in the importance of a cohesive team, imbed that conviction in everything you do. Construct your team with intention and patience. Create collaborative onboarding, involving team members in the selection and training process. Solicit input on key decisions, post-event reviews, and celebrations. Recognize the strengths and motivations of each member, but don't favor any one person. It has to be about the team, not the individuals. If you follow this mantra, others will pick up on it. If you don't, then the team will fall apart in favor of individualism. Consider the team-first approach in every hiring, key decision, team meeting, or action that you take.

Leadership, patience, and consistency are essential. Team chemistry may take time to develop. However, address any glaring issues right away. These might include a lack of a vital skillset, an ongoing clash amongst staff, or a safety or unethical behavior that impinges on an employee's personal rights. These issues should catapult to the top of your list and must be resolved before the environment is ready for a strong team to form.

I've worked on over a dozen teams, many of which I led. The SHAPE Team Building model evolved throughout my career. I've seen many disjointed teams falter and other unified teams excel. Each successful team followed this model. Team shaping takes diligence and persistence. It takes listening skills, caring, and resilience during the long road. It is a pleasure to be part of a team who follows these steps. Successful teams consistently perform better. They attract the best employees, have high retention rates, and exhibit noticeably stronger employee satisfaction.

## Implementing the SHAPE Model

The SHAPE Team Building model sounds simple, but implementation is key. Rarely will you be tasked with assembling a brand-new team. Most of the time you inherit a team. In either case, employ the SHAPE model to assess where your team is and identify gaps. I strongly suggest you not make wholesale changes without careful planning. Rapid adjustments can be an understandable tendency. You may have a vision for the team and a particular style—likely quite different from your predecessor. You want to brand your team and you want to jump into reorganizing and selectively restaffing. You may be correct, yet it is worthwhile to take caution. Many introverts are rather impatient, and determination can quickly become stubbornness. Be aware of this blind spot, consult others, and plan for a successful transition.

## Learning Through Disaster

I want to share one of the most disheartening experiences in my career. Though it turned into a valuable lesson that improved my leadership approach for years to come, I hope you can avoid such a misstep. When I moved from the US to London to lead a global trading team, my manager authorized me to make changes that would elevate the team's productivity and profitability. From office scuttlebutt and my initial discussions with my predecessor, I surmised that I had inherited an experienced yet stale team that was not prepared to meet the challenges of today, let alone the opportunities of the future. I quickly assessed that we needed to make a variety of changes, including reorganizing and replacing numerous staff and supervisors. I thought we needed to shift people to the growing Far Eastern markets, where we were unprepared for the upcoming growth opportunities. Within a few weeks, I began to implement the plan by posting positions around the globe.

It was a disaster. Emboldened by the authority granted to me, I rushed to change without recognizing the sensitivities at play. Though the existing business model may have been stale, my predecessor was beloved by many in the group and throughout the industry. In my rush, I missed the opportunity to listen and learn, and critically to build rapport and trust within the team.

I was blinded by my own introversion. I avoided the stress of engaging with others who, in my quick assessment, were expendable parts of my vision. In my haste, what I did not realize was that I was losing not only the support of the outgoing staff, but more critically the high-performing staff I sought to rebuild around. I failed to elevate caring for others above my impatient drive to deliver. If I had slowed down and dedicated time to listen for the first few months, I might have developed a different strategy. I certainly would have implemented those changes differently, garnering goodwill along the way. Instead, we hastily reorganized. Results eventually improved, but I never accomplished the team dynamics I wanted, and the exceptional success I sought eluded us throughout my three-year tenure.

When you first arrive on the scene, approach this as a project with a timeline. Plot out how you will implement the SHAPE model. Aim to remain open-minded throughout the process. It won't take long for you to assess whether your vision can be achieved by retraining staff, improving communication and coordination, creating clearer objectives through a team goals exercise, or if you need to make further organizational changes. If you determine that staff changes are warranted, sit down and explain them with the team. People will appreciate your professionalism and candor. Any changes, slight or dramatic, can be difficult to implement, but if they are done with care and a long-term vision of the team you wish to lead, the door will be open for you to re-SHAPE your team.

## Team Selection

After you settle into the job and your assessment is complete, you may need to hire people, either as part of your rebuilding plan or due to natural attrition. Approach this opportunity to bring in staff as one of your most sacred responsibilities. Each opening is a chance to fill any skills or personality gaps, improve the diversity of your team, and uplift team chemistry.

When you fill a position, you will likely have to work within corporate guidelines, such as an internal posting system or external services. Augment this required protocol with a personal touch. Gather a list of people to tap on the shoulder and consider encouraging them to apply. You may have built a list from past teams and acquaintances, or from people your team or other co-workers recommend. You can also contact the prospects collected in the spreadsheet described in the HR Planning section of the SHAPE model. Share the posting and grab a coffee. Surprisingly, many people do not scour postings often and they miss out on excellent fits. Introverts are often less likely to raise their hands or pursue prospects, so outreach on your part is generous and may encourage strong candidates to fill glaring gaps in your team. Certainly, you should not show preference during the hiring process, but your personal touch will enrich the bed of candidates.

Once you have prospects, evaluate their applications and résumés and arrange candidate interviews with yourself as well as co-workers and teammates to gain varied perspectives. Identify strong candidates using a mix of questions reviewing aspects of their application, including résumé, interests, and passions. Present scenarios to test their creativity, communication, and thought processes. Provide consistent questions across the pool of candidates to make the evaluation and decision-making process easier. Remember that some candidates may be talkative extroverts and others circumspect introverts who may benefit from a slice of time to ponder questions. Don't let either of these styles, in and of itself, taint a candidacy. Finally, grab an informal coffee with each candidate on the short list to gauge their style, excitement, and concerns in a more relaxed setting.

When you have narrowed your list further, be sure to contact references. Many hiring managers skip this step, convinced of the thoroughness of their process and the scarcity of their time. However, references often shed light on unearthed insights. Probe deeper if you sense any hesitancy or a less than enthusiastic endorsement from a reference. No one's record is spotless. Every style just doesn't mix. It's best to know the issues and shortcomings before making a decision.

Once you hire someone, the decision is yours. You own it—the talent, the teamwork, and the collaboration the new hire brings to the group, as well as the ego, ambition, and competitiveness they may introduce. If the successful candidate fits well and is a strong performer, you can take victory laps, but if they don't, or if their presence turns a good or great organization into a dysfunctional mess, you will own that too. Take your time, seek out different perspectives on the candidates, meet with them again if you have unanswered questions, and let your intuition be your guide. After much consideration, if something doesn't feel right, it probably isn't, and you should move on to another candidate or broaden your search altogether.

## Onboarding Staff

Companies of all sizes neglect onboarding and orientation. Be prepared to supplement any corporate training to create a welcoming transition for the incoming employee, convey core team principles, and provide smooth integration into the team.

Start by reviewing the team's mission, vision, and values (MVV). We will discuss these further in Chapter 15, Culture Creator. This cannot be merely an obligatory check-the-box exercise. Provide background on the development of the MVV, why they are essential, and specific examples of how they have helped guide team members through difficult decisions. Use this opportunity to emphasize the importance of the team over the individual. Share the team's big goals and targets, as well as your expectations of the employee, and finally a transition plan and timeline. Provide ample time for the new team member to get up to speed the right way. Expediency may feel right, but gaps in background, team rapport, and understanding of the rules could become big issues down the road.

Be sure your team member has time with Human Resources, Safety, and Compliance so they are aware of the rules and feel comfortable to refer to these groups when they have questions. You should share your own rigor and approach in each of these areas and emphasize these are the team's license to operate and cannot be undermined.

Encourage each member of your team to grab a casual coffee with the onboarding employee. This is an opportunity for each to build rapport as well as to share their roles and responsibilities and how they may interact in the future. New staff should also meet other important stakeholders, focusing on key internal customers and suppliers before being introduced to outside counterparts.

As an introvert yourself, welcome the fact that everyone has different learning and engagement styles. Your focus should be on integrating the person into the team and building their skillset to accomplish the job, not on their own process or steps for doing so. A purposeful onboarding process will contribute to a smooth transition while conveying priorities of teamwork, creativity, contribution, and compliance.

## Elevating the Team

Many companies focus on how to fill each employee's personal gaps. They send staff to training classes and place goals on their annual performance plan to bridge those gaps. While there may be minimum threshold on certain skills, shift focus toward escalating each person's strengths and passions. Training may nudge a gap forward, but when you help people expand on skills they already enjoy, the yield is exponential.

Facilitate discussions through team personality surveys like Myers-Briggs Type Indicator (MBTI)[32] or team strength assessments like Gallup's Clifton Strengths Finder.[33] You and the team may find that certain tasks fit better with specific people. Leverage everyone's strengths. The team will perform at a higher level when people cover tasks with expertise and zeal for the subject instead of struggling with an assignment they dislike in the first place.

You may feel that this type of exercise is best mandated by you, the manager, perhaps in discussion with each individual team player. Fight this inclination to assign tasks. Offer a bold course to have these discussions as a team. This will promote the team approach and help get everyone on the same page, learning about each other and figuring out how they can support each other. The results can be transformational.

Recognizing strengths and gaps requires self-awareness and vulnerability. When people are asked to identify gaps in interviews, they notoriously draw a blank or offer trite terms like "overworked" or "impatience." It's both mature and liberating to identify and share true gaps that everyone has. People can stop hiding or covering up weaknesses and instead focus on strengths and passion.

Dr. Ty Belknap offers wise advice: "delegating your weaknesses shows your leadership ability."[34] As an example, many introverts struggle with stakeholder engagements. You may tackle these obligations with ambition and determination, but often the interactions lack warmth and bonding. If this is a shortcoming for you, you may align with extroverts on the team to build closer bonds with key stakeholders. You will learn from them and the team will become stronger.

As a generalist, I was thrilled to move around the company. I gained broad experiences and identified best practices that could be transferred around the organization in pursuit of excellence. However, these frequent moves meant I never had the history or detailed expertise that a specialist develops over time. Understanding this gap, I learned to preserve and access such capacity in each team. Identify these stalwarts, learn from them, support their transfer of knowledge, and recognize them in your succession plan.

These important steps help to develop a cohesive, complementary group—a team better prepared to support each other through tough times and to exceed their own expectations together.

## Monitoring and Adjusting

Once you've established a strong team through selection, orientation, and complementary roles, monitor and adjust. I once worked with a manager that liked to put his unknowing team members under stress tests to see how they performed. I'm not an advocate of such devious measures. Work with each team member to develop them personally and professionally. Provide them with support and encouragement as you challenge them with growth opportunities. Employees should not feel like they are under the microscope, but leaders should certainly gauge progress through observation and discussion to best serve the team and each individual.

As soon as days seem to be going smoothly, inevitably an emergency will occur—a conflict within the team arises, a staff member surprises you by resigning, or an unpopular edict appears from upper management that creates a ruckus within the group. These surprises will happen. Expect them. When problems flare up in the team's chemistry, address them before they spread like a wildfire. While the situation may deem you move fast, maintain a calm demeanor. Others will follow the leadership of those that appear to be methodically tackling challenges without losing their cool.

Strong teams don't happen by chance. They require your focus to SHAPE in order to elevate your team to foster creativity, solve problems, and celebrate together.

## ACTIONS:

1. Assess your team's performance through the SHAPE Team Building model: Skills Assessment, HR Planning, Aligned Culture, Perspectives, and Energy. What do you need to shore up?

2. Do you know each team member's strengths? Would the team benefit from reallocating tasks to those who excel and enjoy those tasks more?

Chapter Fifteen

# CULTURE CREATOR

*"Introverts paradoxically pull away from culture and create culture."*
*–Laurie Helgoe, American psychologist with special focus on personalities and culture (1960- )*

As a team leader, one of the most important decisions you make is often the most overlooked: what kind of culture or environment do you want to create for your team? Culture is like branding for your group. Most companies spend considerable thought, time, and money creating a corporate brand which acts as a calling card for stakeholders and investors.

Though your team's brand should not conflict with the company's values, it needs to be customized to fit the purpose and personality of your team. Take liberties to create a brand that is developed by the team and, most importantly, binds all members together and motivates them to success. Your team, no matter how small, will radiate a brand—its own personality and reputation—automatically, so you are much better off proactively crafting it.

Branding cultivates chemistry, creating a sense of pride and ownership within the team. It forms a common framework which all employees, and especially introverts, will find comforting and purposeful. This branding may also represent the team to other internal groups and serve as a recruiting tool for future team members. Who doesn't want to work for a team that is close knit, fun, and successful?

So what is this cultural branding? It's simply the feel within the team. Take a few minutes and think about teams you've worked on before, whether in your same company, at a previous employer, back at school, or at a church or other civic organization. What did you like most about the team and the way the leader conducted the group? Did you feel a sense of camaraderie amongst the team? Do you recall that this particular group was successful?

## Creating and Imbedding an Impactful Culture

Many companies and organizations undergo a mission/vision exercise. You may have participated in several attempts. As you will likely attest, many of these efforts fail. You spend considerable time putting the words together and then there is never any follow through. You never see that mission or vision statement again, and team members mark it up as a frustrating waste of time.

What could possibly make a difference this time? Creating and imbedding an impactful culture follows a three-step process of championing the effort, incorporating team participation, and following through by engraining the mission and vision within your team.

1. **Mission Possible:** As the leader you must believe in and champion the process. Reflect on past groups you worked on. Cohesive, successful, and enjoyable teams don't happen by accident. They arise from intentional leadership. Develop a mission and vision exercise that you are committed to using by applying common introvert strengths like creativity, thoughtfulness, and listening skills. Believing in the value of the program and sharing other successful experiences will encourage the team to consider the possibilities. Respect your team's time and be patient for the results to develop in a relaxed and creative atmosphere.

   Teambuilding exercises can fail if you haven't assembled the right personalities and chemistry through team selection. Most often, failure results from the hesitance and less-than-enthusiastic commitment of the leader. You are key to the team's success.

2. **Creating Together:** Establish your team's vision and mission. Bain & Company, a leading corporate consultant, recaps the components as "A **Mission Statement** defines the company's business, its **objectives** and its approach to reach those objectives. A **Vision Statement** describes the desired **future** position of the company. Elements of Mission and Vision Statements are often combined to provide a statement of the company's purposes, goals and values."[35] Encapsulating a team's dreams and objectives in one sentence can often empower people to focus and achieve great things.

   Most importantly, this is a team exercise. This is not about presenting *your* vision and mission to the team, no matter how crisp it may sound. The true value of the program is that everyone is involved, and that the full team owns the ultimate product. Many organizations spend hours or even weeks crafting a statement. I encourage you to prune back the non-essentials and target a concise process. Break the exercise into distinct segments so they don't become overbearing, at which point the creativity and brainstorming energy will fade.

Set up an initial meeting at a relaxed venue, perhaps at a restaurant's private room, outside on your campus, or during an off-campus away-day. Try to have all team members join face-to-face for the initial meeting. After icebreakers that are enjoyable for even the most reserved participants, explain why you believe a mission and vision is so important and that you are going to make this exercise fun and effective in three easy steps:

1) Start by asking everyone to jot down on small pieces of paper or sticky notes a few words about **what product or service the team delivers,** thus describing the team's primary objective. Recall the five functions of a group as described in Chapter 11: Money Maker, Cost Saver, Creative Innovator, Functional Expert, and People Leader. Consider how your team meets the needs of your customers through these functions. Give each person time to process the request thoughtfully and develop their list without any immediate pressure to present. These notes form the basis of a mission that drives the team every day.

2) Next, consider **what the vision of the future is for your team**. Look at your goals and dreams. Consider the current and projected state of your business and industry. A brief presentation on the state of the industry and new trends shared by yourself or ideally an outside expert, will spark

the discussions. What will change and how do you foresee your team positioning itself to succeed in that future? Are you producing innovative products or technology, improving efficiency, expanding territory? This set of sticky notes guides your team's future.

3) Finally, and perhaps most importantly, ask everyone to jot down a few thoughts on the **type of environment they want to work in**. What values do they want the team to represent? You may hear words or phrases including learning environment, feedback culture, work/life balance, creativity, transparency, collaboration, reliability, or risk-taking, as well as fun, trusting, collaborative, and a team others seek to join.

By the time you complete this three-step process, the room will likely be buzzing with energy. Once you collect these three sets of notes, start with the first and encourage the team to narrow them by eliminating duplicates and then challenging any they don't believe belong. Don't get bogged down in assessing your current state of business and the gaps to reach your mission, vision, and values. There will be time for that later. Before the energy level starts to fade, wrap up the session and move on. Ask the team to pick the top three suggestions for each: mission, vision, and values (MVV).

As the leader, you guide the process, but it should be highly interactive. You surely have your own thoughts but remain open-minded and encourage team member ideas along the way. You need to find alignment, not only for this exercise but to keep the full team working together on the same objectives every day. With broadminded consideration and tactful debate, you can land on the principles that represent the vision of both your team and its leader.

I suggest ending this session on a high note. Ask for feedback from participants and share your pleasure with the energy level as well as your commitment to complete the process and imbed the results within the team. The next aspect, perhaps the hardest and most tedious, is crafting the remaining words into three statements. Enlist a small group of volunteers to take a crack at pulling the words together over the next week or two, in time for your next scheduled team meeting. These three statements will become your mission, vision, and values—together, your team's culture.

3. **Integrate Your Message:** The third step in the process is to begin to integrate the mission, vision, and values in everything you do. People spent quality time on these statements, and they reflect your objectives and the culture you want to create and maintain. As a team, spend time assessing your current state of business relative to the MVV you have all created. Focus on bridging these gaps will validate the investment your team made in this exercise, and more importantly will transform your team together.

   Keep your MVV alive and relevant for the team. Sara Bonario, the Director of Renewable Fuels, notes: "I think the key is bringing it down from 30,000 feet into the heart of the team so each individual owns it and lives by it." Include the team's MVV on emails, post them in your team's work area, and incorporate them in your meeting agendas. Use them to challenge the work the team is doing. If you have projects or meetings that are not in line with your MVV, evaluate whether they can be skipped or minimized. If the values the team selected are not being adhered to by the team or any member including yourself, address that either as a team or through individual coaching. Encouraging this discussion and challenge is essential to keeping a cohesive team on track. Your three pronouncements should act as guides and empower everyone to challenge any items that might conflict with these statements. The power of these declarations is not in the words, but how they are implemented going forward. You will know your efforts to entrench your culture are working if you ask others in the organization to describe your team and their answers match the mission, vision, and values you have strived to imbed.

Many companies conduct annual surveys to gauge how the organization is performing in creating a positive work environment. Unfortunately, surveys don't often drill down to the smaller team level. If yours does not, create a brief, anonymous survey to poll the team on how the group and its leader are performing in line with the mission, vision, and values established. After you have time to reflect, discuss the findings, seek comments, and note steps you will take to advance the team to the next level.

Sustaining a strong team culture takes a lot of work. It demands integrating the mission, vision, and values in every hire, coaching session, and team meeting you have. It requires soliciting feedback and making corrections. It certainly entails ownership by all team members starting with yourself. With fortitude, the culture created will continue to flourish and evolve, transcending well beyond the tenure of its current leadership.

## Meeting the Challenge

Team meetings are an essential way to integrate your culture. After all, these are opportunities when the full team is together. Use them wisely, but don't abuse them. Make special effort to give remote team members the opportunity to build rapport with others and include them in meeting discussions as often as possible.

As a team leader, you will lead meetings focused on objectives from coaching staff to setting annual goals. All will play a role in supporting your mission, vision, and values.

## Full Team Meetings

Remember that these are *team* meetings, not *team leader* meetings. Everyone appreciates a gathering with a variety of speakers, topics, and styles rather than simply listening to the leader drone on. Structure the meeting to include everyone's participation, including introvert and extrovert, sage veteran and newest addition. Take the opportunity in advance to tap others to present topics or share a success, best practice, or learning. Avoid the monotony of dry speeches from the front of the room. Include roundtable discussions and breakout sessions if practical. Each team member is likely involved in many meetings each week. Make sure your full team meetings are fun, efficient, and participative events people look forward to.

A team meeting is your most reliable, routine way to get everyone together. People want to be part of a mission, to have a purpose. Solicit team members for agenda items and then share the itinerary and any pre-read in advance, along with questions or decisions to be addressed. These actions will foster better discussions amongst introverts and extroverts alike. A standard agenda may include:

- Updates and successes presented by team member(s)
- Team metrics which tie to your mission or vision (e.g., sales numbers, efficiency data)
- Obstacles to success for the team to problem solve together
- Policy or procedural updates that can't be conveyed by email
- Recognition of team members linked to examples supporting the mission, vision, and values
- Insight regarding upper management's tone and priorities along with your view of how these may impact your team.

Solicit questions from the team. Answer with vulnerability, compassion, and transparency. Team meetings provide a unique path toward closer bonding and team chemistry for all involved, certainly including the team leader.

## One-on-One Meetings

I suggest that you schedule a one-hour meeting every two weeks with each of your team members. Either of you can place items on the itinerary, ranging from a periodic performance review to an update on a project or a casual check-in on how things are going. This type of meeting is often an ideal structure for introverts who crave more intimate settings with agendas and purpose. You can use the time to discuss their career development and ambitions, or to provide training focused on expanding their strengths. Sometimes you may need more time to complete a topic and other times you will not need the full hour. Scheduling these meetings helps you remain aligned, allows you to monitor any potential issues, and shows respect for their time and calendar. Give these meetings a priority on your calendar. Cancelling them without an emergency will send a message that your time together is no longer important to you, and the rapport you've created will start to wither.

## Team Away Days

Teams often overlook the value of Away Days—typically two to three-day getaways where the whole team goes off-campus to discuss business roles and goals, and most importantly enjoy casual team bonding.

They can be elaborate road trips to resorts or beaches or simply planned retreats just across town. Yet the value remains. Away Days can be daunting experiences for many introvert leaders. They feel dreadfully social, with the spotlight on you. To soften the pressure, focus on your teambuilding objectives to create a comfortable atmosphere. Ask others to help plan the event and lead certain sessions. Beware of asking the same people to arrange them—there's a real problem with giving underrepresented groups the "housekeeping" tasks. Shine the spotlight on others. Provide time during each day for everyone to relax and recharge. Being kind to yourself and taking full advantage of these breaks will help maintain a high energy level for everyone.

## Tips for Great Away Days

1. Work with the team to develop an agenda in advance;
2. Involve many team members to share topics and lead sessions;
3. Invite an internal partner or outside customer as a guest speaker to provide perspective;
4. Offer plenty of breaks, especially if office work must still be done;
5. Schedule at least one-third of the time to be social teambuilding;

6. Avoid cheesy icebreakers, but consider team personality tests (Myers-Briggs) or strength-based quizzes (Gallup Clifton) to discover and share each person's forte and how the team may become stronger. These sessions encourage vulnerability and can catapult team chemistry and collaboration. Whether you facilitate the session or bring in HR to help, be prepared to share your personal perspectives first to break the ice.

7. Host a unique dinner. Toast each team member by recognizing one of their accomplishments. If you include drinks, choose a venue within walking distance or use taxi services.

## Celebratory Team Outings

These can be as simple as a team breakfast or mid-day coffee, or as extensive as a celebratory team dinner with spouses. Celebrations are a great way to share successes across the team and brag about each person with their spouse or significant other proudly watching. Flex your creative and planning skills to assemble a memorable event or enlist team members to help pull it off. The event doesn't have to be formal or expensive. People remember unique events best. Try a family kickball game and cookout, or an Italian or Caribbean dinner including themed attire and decorations. Host the team and significant others at your home for dinner and games. The options are only limited by the imagination of yourself and the team.

Each of these meetings and gatherings build your team as one cohesive unit. Feedback affirms these make a critical difference and deserve to be a priority for every leader.

## ACTIONS:

1. How would you describe your team's culture – productive, collaborative, and fun or disjointed and chaotic?

2. Does each team member know your group's mission, vision, and values?

3. Do you use each of the four meeting types throughout the year?

Chapter Sixteen

# TEAM COACH

*"Hail to the man who went through life always helping others,*
*knowing no fear, and to whom aggressiveness and resentment*
*are alien. Such is the stuff of which the great moral leaders are*
*made."*
*–Albert Einstein, considered one of the greatest physicists of all*
*time (1879-1955)*

Introverts often steer away from being coaches. They see coaching as fraught with conflict and spontaneous debate. With this mindset, it's a wonder anyone except the most extreme extrovert would approach coaching. However, being a team coach is a critical function of every leader and offers the satisfaction and pride of stretching yourself to make a positive impact on others. You are much more prepared for the role than you might think. Your strengths and mindset can make you a powerful coach to support your team members through their own career journey.

Although coaching certainly requires us to develop and flex less familiar muscles, the focus should not be upon us, but rather on those we are coaching. How can we help them to excel? How can we support discovery of their own strengths, styles, and motivation? How can we build their confidence to succeed? How can we help them build their own toolkit to flourish in the various situations discussed in Section II and perhaps become a leader for tomorrow? The answers lie in your own courage and resiliency. Provide valuable feedback even if it is difficult and be flexible even when it places added pressure and responsibility upon yourself.

## Exerting Your Superpowers

Key attributes of successful coaches include preparation, thoughtfulness, empathy, listening, and resilience. The best coaches, whether at work or in sports, prepare for the game, listen to their players, and inspire through thoughtful consideration of each individual player's strengths and motivations. Bill Belichick, renowned New England Patriots head football coach, professed: "I think everyone is a case-by-case basis. Whatever the circumstances are that come with any individual, they exist and you have to make a determination as to what your comfort level is with that person and the characteristics that they bring." Coaches, whether in sports or in the office, can offer this individualized guidance through listening and observation.

Don't rush coaching opportunities. They are the essence of the leadership role. With care and patience, you will make a difference for your team members and you will learn along the way. These tools will help you manage the most challenging conversations in a caring way that delivers results. Your resilience will enable you to deal with the inevitable, yet unforeseeable, bumps.

In this final leadership chapter, we will cover three types of coaching: mastering the difficult conversation, cultivating ongoing coaching, and nurturing career development discussions. Each contributes to the support and development of team members, and each requires different skills to make a positive difference.

## Mastering the Difficult Conversation

Dealing with a disgruntled team member? Addressing staff conflict that risks team chemistry? Coaching staff toward improved performance?

Difficult situations at work are inevitable, but the conversations about them are not. Many leaders recoil from these uncomfortable discussions. Yet these are often the most significant exchanges you will have with your team members. Avoiding the dialogue means you and your staff are missing the opportunity to learn and grow together. Both parties are apprehensive, but both parties know that sweeping issues under the rug usually just allows the problem to fester and grow, becoming a cancer on the team and stunting the progress of the team member you have been obliged to develop.

Okay, so you should not avoid these conversations, but how do you tackle them?

## An Example: Seeking Performance Improvement

Early in my first supervisory job, Bill, a gasoline truck driver on my team in Detroit, was clearly not meeting expectations. Our efficiency reports showed he consistently delivered fewer loads from our terminal to the local gas stations than any of the other two dozen drivers. He hung around the terminal too long and spent too much time at the station chatting with the managers after he completed his delivery. I began to see the trend in our reports but hesitated to address the issue. I was a recent arrival to the Detroit plant, while Bill had been hauling gasoline in Detroit longer than I'd been alive. He was ornery and apt to bring issues to his local union representative. Perhaps the problem was overblown? Maybe it would correct itself? Maybe his fellow drivers would discuss the issue and together resolve the problem? I waited.

Finally, one of the drivers pulled me aside and said they were annoyed that Bill was slacking and the other drivers had to pull his loads. He asked what I was going to do about it. "Do your job!" he insisted. I recognized that my laissez-faire approach was contributing to the problem.

When the day was over, I asked Bill to come into my office. Without any prelude, I laid out the issue. Bill immediately erupted. "I've been doing this a long time. How long have you been here? Have you ever ridden with me to see what I do? I haul plenty of gasoline, in the rain and snow, in bad traffic. It's exhausting and stressful, but I do it. And yes, I do talk to the station owners. They trust me! Most of our drivers don't even know their names."

I was flat-footed. This barrage left me flustered and out of control. All I could do was repeat the issue: "I need you to haul your share of the loads. Others have noticed and have brought it up. The delivery reports show that you haul fewer loads per day than any other driver." This didn't calm the room, much less solve the issue. After another round of debate, I finally made my first good decision of the day: I suggested we break and talk again after his next shift in a few days.

When Bill left, I closed the door and collapsed into my chair. What a mess! After a while, I collected myself. I knew I had bungled the meeting. I had been ill prepared for the long overdue discussion. I couldn't just leave the issue now. I had to change my approach. I met with my manager to share the debate and seek sage advice. I talked to one of the other terminal supervisors that had previously managed Bill and the driver fleet. I considered their valuable input and jotted down my new approach, practiced my points, and envisioned the next conversation. When Bill and I met again, I began to follow my process, which I later dubbed **The 8 Rs**:

1. **Rapport Building:** I had failed to get to know Bill in the weeks since my arrival at the terminal. Now I needed to dig out of the hole I'd made. At our follow up meeting, I started with general conversation and asked questions about Bill's family and hobbies. I shared my discomfort from our previous discussion and told Bill I'd like to start over. I certainly would have benefited from building this rapport with Bill when I first arrived, but my new efforts appeared genuine and did help to defuse the situation.

2. **Raise the Issue in a Confident Yet Clear Manner:** My aim was to be empathetic but also be confident. These are not mutually exclusive. At the end of the day, I was trying to solve a problem and change performance. "Let's talk about the delivery process. I'm pretty new here and I want to support you and the other drivers. You know the terminal is under a lot of pressure to perform. I want to learn how I can help you. We both want the same things."

3. **Request Ideas and Suggestions:** This time I aimed to be open-minded. There are always two sides to every story, and the truth often lies somewhere in the middle. "Bill, how can we get more aligned? I'd like to better understand what you and the other drivers do." Bill suggested I join him on a delivery or two. I thought it was a great idea and we planned a day for

the following week. During the ride we got to know each other, and he shared his duties and the risks of delivering gasoline.

4. **Reveal Vulnerabilities:** Our ride-along offered me the chance to soften the conversation, so I opted to let my guard down and share a few of my own goals and fears. I voiced my genuine excitement about working at the plant because "this is where the work truly happens." I also shared my honest apprehension because everything was unfamiliar, and I had a lot to learn. We grew to appreciate each other's perspective and wanted to help each other succeed.

5. **Ripen Solutions:** During the ride, I was able to casually re-introduce the issue. I chose to soften the reference to reports, but I still led with facts. "Bill, over time you are not pulling the same number of loads as others. The rest of the fleet looks up to you as a leader. You are a role model." I paused and later added: "I understand and support the need for breaks, and I think the rapport you've built with the station managers is essential. How do you think we can solve this issue?"

6. **Regroup Together on Solutions:** Bill understood the pressures the terminal was under and was proud of his role as a leader. He recognized my more open approach. Bill then proposed to limit his breaks to the norm of fifteen minutes between loads so he could haul another load and still have a few minutes to touch base with each station manager. I shared my appreciation and support for his idea. We had struck a mutually beneficial pact.

7. **Relax and Exert Patience:** It took two meetings and a road trip with Bill to accomplish my objective. In the end, performance improved, and I had a much greater appreciation for what Bill and the other drivers do. I would not have achieved either

if I had insisted on pushing my agenda through in an office meeting.

8. **Review Performance:** I continued to monitor the reports, but more importantly I touched base with Bill often and rode with him again every quarter. I also introduced quarterly drives with each of the other drivers, helping to build relationships, change the culture, and improve performance. Not only were the issues with Bill rectified, but others also noticed the difference. Driver efficiency improved and word spread of my curiosity and empathy.

## Lessons Learned

I hope you recognize the chance to approach these coaching opportunities like any of the other challenges we've covered in this section. Lean on your strengths and values and come with the proper mindset. In the first conversation with Bill, I was not prepared. I was spouting off statistics and hearsay. I didn't ask questions and our conversation suffered from a lack of rapport. It took a lot of concerted effort to build a bridge with Bill and address the issue because of my poor display during our first meeting, but I invested the time to foster a positive relationship.

In this instance, coaching started with listening but also included brainstorming solutions, developing alignment, and monitoring progress. Coaching does not have to be a lecture or a class instructional. The best coaching feels like a two-way discussion that accomplishes the main objective without either party feeling coerced.

We all like good news and for everything to go as planned, but these difficult conversations are what leaders are called upon to do. Avoiding these moments doesn't make you a leader at all. Managing these tough discussions is a prerequisite for good leadership. Through practice these discussions help you to become a great leader.

My assignment in Detroit was my first supervisory role after six years in corporate staff jobs. Having such an early opportunity to learn and grow my leadership skills was invaluable. Doing so in a field location stripped of much of the protocol and polish of corporate head office was an extra reward. Throughout my ensuing years of team leadership, I often reflected upon my two years in Detroit and the lessons I learned from Bill and others.

## Employing Effective Coaching Techniques

Coaching is more than just rising to the challenge of a difficult conversation. It involves daily support for each team member. Start by setting purposeful goals with each team member – specific targets, skills to develop, relationships to build. Then help them discover how to best accomplish those goals. Begin with listening. Brainstorm together, encourage their ideas, and provide suggestions, but don't preach. No one likes a lecture, even if it is filled with wisdom.

During the exchange, look for learning for yourself as well as systemic issues that may need attention across the team, whether through your training or coaching process or in the procedures binding all staff.

Utilize your team as a coaching mechanism. Connect people who are trying to develop particular skills with others who have mastered those talents. Include a Leadership Moment section in your staff meetings for team members to share topics like how to work more efficiently, how to build rapport with challenging coworkers or customers, and how to negotiate under pressure.

For instance, one of my team members led a discussion on multi-tasking with the team, concluding that although it appeared to be the cultural norm, multi-tasking sacrificed focus and delivery. This realization instantly changed how everyone conducted their business. This forum was extremely helpful in getting ideas on the table from diverse perspectives, and it gave me an opportunity to drop in suggestions without the session feeling like a lecture. This team approach to coaching didn't deflect my responsibilities, but enhanced them.

## Nurturing Career Development

Coaching is not just about performance improvement. It applies to staff career development as well. Jay Artale, the former Executive Director at Sony, reflected: "The manager I had the most respect for was the one who focused on career development. When somebody was in the wrong role, he shuffled them around… Moving people to new roles is a journey, and it's one that you and your team member[s] have to do together." Everyone benefits from such connection and guidance—including the team and organization.

## Career Development Partnership

I've met many managers who only focus on delivery of their team goals. They have little interest in their staff's future career paths. Certain managers fear that talking about career development detracts from focus on delivering now. They worry people will be quick to rush off to the next opportunity, just when they have been trained. Others have even blocked team members from applying for other roles outside of their group. These are the very managers that must deal with low job satisfaction and high employee turnover.

People will leave the team or the company if their needs aren't met. Why? Because our team members are no different than ourselves. They naturally have one eye toward their future. They want to be sure there is an intriguing role ahead that provides challenge and personal financial growth. Introverts, in particular, may feel unsettled without a plan and progress toward that career path. Effective leaders link their team member's current job with their aspirations by focusing on the skills and experiences they need to develop now to support their future ambitions.

Leaders should leverage their experience to provide a combination of feedback and input into each team member's career development journey. Career development and job search should be a partnership between the leader and each team member.

## Skills Development

Each team is made up of unique individuals. Provide personalized attention. Foster discussions to learn about their strengths, motivations, and dreams. How do these align with their career plans? Identify those key skills necessary to succeed in their current role, as well as their prospective career ambitions, and provide an honest assessment of their development. You both will then be able to focus on developing those skills through experience and further coaching.

Though there may be minimum thresholds for various skills, people will grow significantly by focusing on strengths rather than gaps. Help expand these strengths by providing specific, prompt coaching. Immediately after a meeting or project, review how the team member performed relative to the strengths they are working to expand. This coaching can be magnified by providing subject matter role models and specific work tasks to practice skills, whether they are leadership, communications, or decision-making.

Give people opportunities to gain unique skills and experiences they will need to progress. For example, if your team works closely with a distribution plant or particular product, arrange field trips to expose staff to these items so they may appreciate how these facets interact with other parts of the business. It's a great way to expand their network and possibly their career interests.

Provide leadership opportunities that may include supervising temporary workers, summer interns, or project teams. Many people may have innate leadership instincts, but all leaders learn through mistakes and successes.

## Job Search Advocate

Incorporate conversations about career interests in your routine one-on-one meetings. Encourage people to think broadly across the organization. Illuminate how skills and interests can be applied in a variety of roles. Put team members in contact with managers and role models throughout the organization so they can scope out prospective roles and build a broader, deeper network.

Some people are anxious to move too quickly. Others find it hard to leave a job and team where they feel comfortable. The timeframe for advancing should start when someone has gained critical, unique skills, delivered consistently on and above their goals, and has built the strengths necessary to compete for prospective roles.

Finally, be an active part of their job search. Help your people expand their networks. Review their résumés or other internal documents and job applications. Provide tips and guidance. Be a strong reference while also networking behind the scenes. Be as flexible as you can with timing when your staff does secure their next role. Transitions are challenging so flexibility is always appreciated.

Coaching, both for performance and career development, is not only where you earn your stripes, but also where you may find the greatest pride and job satisfaction. Use your strengths and values to treat people with honesty, respect, and support. Coaching is about continually learning. No one is perfect and you will make mistakes. The key is to grow from them. Be honest and authentic in your communication, and you will earn the respect that every leader needs to succeed.

## ACTIONS:

1.  If you are a team leader, difficult conversations are inevitable. Review your most recent conversations using **The 8 Rs**. Prepare for the next challenging discussion with those same guidelines in mind.

2.  Are you reinforcing each team member efforts to accomplish purposeful goals? Are you engaging with them regularly and also providing role models, mentors, and opportunities to develop and practice new skills?

3.  Are you supporting each team member's career ambitions? Are you both aligned on key strengths to develop further and are you providing the feedback and experiences necessary for their growth?

4.  Are you supporting team member's aspirations and applications for their next assignment through coaching, references, and flexibility?

Chapter Seventeen

# THE INTROVERT'S
# MANIFESTO

*"The formula of happiness and success is just being actually*
*yourself, in the most vivid possible way you can."*
*–Meryl Streep, often described as the "best actress of her*
*generation" (1949- )*

We may look upon our mature neighborhood tree as a
magnificent, strong, and perhaps daunting figure. We can lose
sight of the roots below and the nourishment and time needed for
a sapling to eventually reach its impressive vastness. Yet, over
time and with the right nutrients, roots bloom into trees, trunks
grow sturdy, branches expand to outstanding heights, and the tree
eventually blossoms and returns the gift of life to the earth through
seedlings upon the land around it.

So, too, is an introvert's journey. We dream of the beauty and contributions we can provide to our workplace and community, yet sometimes we feel those are unattainable for us. Yet the world is ripe for our contributions.

Introverts worldwide are shedding the negative stereotypes that have held so many back for so long. Now you are prepared to travel your introvert journey—to know yourself, apply your authenticity, find the right fit, and lead with humility and confidence.

In Section One, we explored your roots: strengths, values, and mindsets. These teachings apply to your whole life. The talents you discovered enable you to get out from behind the mask and be a more confident and determined person, both at work and at home. The strengths you hold are vital in every business, providing diverse perspectives and approaches that empower companies to succeed in the decades ahead. I want to challenge you to grow your strengths, proclaim your introversion, and proudly lead your way.

In Section Two, we covered how to apply your talents, mindset, and ambitions to grow each branch. Suddenly, imposing obstacles like uncertainty, communications, meetings, and networking have become your constructive breeding ground for ideas and relationships. By successfully navigating these challenges, your confidence grows and makes your dreams and ambitions possible.

Section Three focused on cultivating an opportune environment for sustainable growth by finding the right organization and team in which you can thrive. This starts by developing alignment and collaboration with your manager and others to develop your career path. Be sure you are planting your roots with a manager and organization that can help you flourish.

Section Four provided the framework to become an inspirational leader, a wise tree leading the teams of today and sowing the leaders of tomorrow. Teams want supervisors who are courageous, vulnerable, and authentic. These are your traits. These are your superpowers. When you apply authenticity, along with a dose of compassion and confidence, your team will bond together and achieve amazing results.

Stand tall, lean on your strengths, and lead your way. I encourage you to lead by example, advocating for yourself and others in order to bring more diversity and respect to the workplace.

The following is *The Introvert's Manifesto*. It serves as a declaration of many introvert capabilities and aspirations. I invite you to consider each decree, modify them as necessary to reflect your own strengths, mindsets, and ambitions, and embrace them as your own personal philosophy, a reminder of who you are and how you operate. You may choose to share tenets of your platform with your manager or discuss the entire Manifesto to create further alignment and understanding. Or you may just choose to post them privately, but embrace them and be inspired by them daily.

## The Introvert's Manifesto

**I do like people.** I may not be the loudest or the most engaging person in the room, but I do enjoy time with other people. I prefer the time in short segments and in smaller groups.

**It's nothing personal.** My energy does drain during the day, especially from extended social interactions. I just need to recharge periodically. Sometimes I need a walk around the office or campus or grab lunch by myself to reenergize.

**I am ambitious.** I have career goals and aspirations. I may seem reticent, but I love to deliver. I take pride in my work, I want to succeed, and I want to progress. Judge me for my accomplishments, not for my lack of verbosity.

**I am an avid learner.** I learn through observation and analysis. I relish the wisdom of role models, leaders, and mentors. I am humble yet confident enough to seek feedback and coaching. I thrive on the opportunity to expand my comfort zone and stretch kindly.

**I love to contribute.** I don't usually jump into debates or have a quick-handed comment, but I want to contribute. I pride myself on being prepared for meetings, strategy sessions, and conferences. I book preparation time on my calendar so I can do my homework ahead of time, consider all sides of an issue, and come ready to bring valuable perspectives and recommendations to the table.

**I can develop strong relationships.** As an introvert, though I may appear to retain a quiet demeanor, I'm primed to develop deeper relationships over time. I am driven to succeed, and I like to develop work teams, project teams, and customer relationships in my own way. I thrive in small groups where I can really get to know someone: what makes them tick, their motivators, their personal interests. And as I build this rapport, I can leverage this to deliver value for everyone.

**I have a strong risk appetite.** I don't typically speak impulsively. That feels like hasty risk to me. But if I have time to evaluate a situation, analyze pros and cons, develop fallback options, and plan my approach, I love to put my money where my mouth is and advocate prudent risk. I'm especially analytical and will want to track progress and consider lessons learned afterward.

**I am a loyal team member.** Don't assume I only want to work independently. While I do like working alone, I also perform well with teams that respect each other and provide space for a diverse range of thought, including introversion. I am an uber-loyalist and work hard to complement and lead a strong, cohesive team. I want to be paid a fair wage, but occasional recognition and job fulfillment are what keep me going every day.

**I am a valued part of your team.** Many managers now recognize the tremendous value of diversity—diversity of background and experience. It is most powerful to combine such a mixture with diversity of thought and perspective. I can provide caution to other's affinity for spontaneous reactions. I spark creativity, empathy, and authenticity, as well as a balanced approach to problem solving. I will advocate for teams to make space for this diversity of thought and perspective as well.

**I will be a great leader.** Leaders are not just the ones who are charming socialites or who command the room through orations and rhetoric. I am great at getting to know my teammates one-on-one. I plan and strategize. I am resilient under pressure and I am secure enough to ask questions and solicit help. And perhaps most of all, I empathize with others and leverage the strengths of everyone to form cohesive teams that deliver great value. I will work hard to develop my skills and be worthy of the opportunity to lead.

You are now equipped with your most important leadership tool: confidence in yourself. Alert to your own superpowers, centered by your mindset focus, and driven by your passion and ambition, you now have the self-confidence to not only achieve the Contentment phase of introversion many aspire to, but to flourish as a person and a leader.

Follow your own Manifesto.* Encourage others to join the introvert revolution. Stand tall and be confident in your strengths. Reach for the sky. Our past may have been filled with struggles and anxieties, but now your future is unlimited. Why wait? The time is ripe. Lead and thrive with confidence.

*Personalize your own Introvert's Manifesto by downloading at www.BeyondIntroversion.com/tci-landing-page.

# REFERENCES

1   Steve Friedman, "Answers Lie in the Science of the Introvert's Brain," Beyond Introversion, 2021, https://beyondintroversion. com/post/answers-lie-in-the-science-of-the-introvert-s-brain

2   Dr. Nick Venters, "The past, present and future of innovation in mental health," NHS Digital, 2018, https://digitial.nhs.uk/blog/transformation-blog/2018/ the-past-present-and-future-of-innovation-in-mental-health

3   Tana Ososki, "Introversion is Environmental," The Rubicon, 2019, https://www.rubiconline.com/ two-sides-one-story-is-introversion-genetic-or-environmental/

4   u/Paco_the_finesser, "Have you ever felt like an outcast?", Reddit, 2017, https://www.reddit.com/r/introvert/ comments/67kcn2/have_you_ever_felt_like_an_outcast/

5   Shaunigan, "The Introversion to extroversion continuum," StrengthsMining, 2014, https://www.strengthsmining. com/2014/03/the-introversion-to-extroversion-continuum/

6   Steve Friedman, "US Presidents Who Were Introverts (and what makes them great)," Introvert, Dear, 2020, https://introvertdear.com/news/ united-states-presidents-who-were-introverts/

7   "How Understanding Your Values Can Make You More Confident," Success Rockets, 2018, https://successrockets.com/understanding-values-make-you-confident/

8   John Maxwell, from "Cleaning Up Your Mental Mess with Dr. Caroline Leaf," The John Maxwell Leadership Podcast, March 3, 2021

9   MindTools.com, "What are Your Values?" MindTools.com, 2016, https://www.mindtools.com/pages/article/newTED_85.htm

10  Kristin Neff, *Self-Compassion: The Proven Power of Being Kind to Yourself* (Williams Morrow: New York, 2011), back cover

11  Gill Hasson, *Mindfulness: Be Mindful. Live in the Moment.* (Fall River Press: New York, 2013), page 90

12  Lesley Sword, "The Gifted Introvert," Gifted & Creatives Services, 2000, http://www.americanacademyk8.org/aastaffhome/BOD/forms/sss/TheGiftedIntrovert.pdf

13  Dr. Ty Belknap, *Leadership for Introverts: The Power of Quiet Influence* (Tacoma, Washington, Port Bell, Inc, 2018), page 171

14  Karen Wickre, *Taking the Work Out of Networking: Your Guide to Making and Keeping Great Connections* (New York, Gallery Books, 2018)

15  Jennifer Kahnweiler, *The Introverted Leader: Building on Your Quiet Strength* (Berrett-Koehler Publishers, Inc., Oakland, CA, 2018), page 32

16  Alicia Dale, "Introverts Excel in Sales," Beyond Introversion blog, 2021, https://www.beyondintroversion.com/post/introverts-excel-in-sales

17  Rainer Strack, Carsten von der Linden, Mike Booker, and Andrea Strohmayr, "Decoding Global Talent," Boston Consulting Group, 2014, https://www.bcg.com/publications/2014/people-organization-human-resources-decoding-global-talent

18  Beth Thornton, "7 Statistics You Can't Ignore About Leadership Development," Inspire, 2018, https://blog.inspiresoftware.com/7-statistics-leadership-development

19  Kathy Caprino, "The Changing Face Of Leadership: 10 New Research Findings All Leaders Need To Understand," Forbes, 2018, https://www.forbes.com/sites/kathycaprino/2018/02/28/the-changing-face-of-leadership-10-new-research-findings-all-leaders-need-to-understand/

20  Kristin Myers, "Americans are Retiring at an Increasing Pace," Yahoo!Finance, 2018, https://finance.yahoo.com/news/americans-retiring-increasing-pace Chapter Title

21  Jeanne Meister, "The Future Of Work: Job Hopping Is the 'New Normal' for Millennials," Forbes, 2012, https://www.forbes.com/sites/jeannemeister/2012/08/14/the-future-of-work-job-hopping-is-the-new-normal-for-millennials

22  Anthony Caruso, "Statistics of U.S. Businesses Employment and Payroll Summary: 2012," United States Census Bureau, 2015

23  Gyzel Pialat, "Future-Proofing Leaders for 2030 and Beyond White Paper," STRATX ExL, https://www.stratx-exl.com/industry-insights/future-proof-leaders-whitepaper

24  Arthur Zuckerman, "37 Leadership Statistics: 2019/2020 Data, Trends & Predictions," Compare, 2020, https://comparecamp.com/leadership-statistics/

25  Christopher J. Brooks, "Why so many black business professionals are missing from the C-suite," CBSNews.com, 2019, https://www.cbsnews.com/news/black-professionals-hold-only-3-percent-of-executive-jobs-1-percent-of-ceo-jobs-at-fortune-500-firms-new-report-says/

26  Pete Ross, "If You're an Introvert, You're Probably Getting Screwed at Work," Observer, 2017, https://observer.com/2017/01/introverts-underrepresented-managerial-positions/

27  Ibid

28  Arthur Zuckerman, "37 Leadership Statistics: 2019/2020 Data, Trends & Predictions," Compare, 2020, https://comparecamp.com/leadership-statistics/

29  Gyzel Pialat, "Future-Proofing Leaders for 2030 and Beyond White Paper," STRATX ExL, https://www.stratx-exl.com/industry-insights/future-proof-leaders-whitepaper

30  Steve Friedman, "Answers Lie in the Science of the Introvert's Brain," Beyond Introversion, 2021, https://beyondintroversion.com/post/answers-lie-in-the-science-of-the-introvert-s-brain

31  APS, "Why Introverts Shy Away From Leadership," Association for Psychological Science, 2017, https://www.psychologicalscience.org/news/minds-business/

research-shows-why-introverts-shy-away-from-leadership.
html

32 https://www.mbtionline.com/

33 https://www.gallup.com/cliftonstrengths

34 Dr. Ty Belknap, *Leadership for Introverts: The Power of Quiet Influence* (Tacoma, Washington, Port Bell, Inc, 2018), page 221

35 "Mission and Vision Statements," Bain & Company, 2018, www.bain.com/insights/ management-tools-mission-and-vision-statements

# ADDITIONAL RESOURCES

Each of these books or resources has contributed in a tangible way to my own thinking and development as an introverted leader. If specific passages or quotations were used, they are referenced in the endnotes. I encourage you to consider making these references part of your own growth library.

- Dr. Ty Belknap, *Leadership for Introverts: The Power of Quiet Influence* (Tacoma, WA, Port Bell, Inc.), 2018.
- Brené Brown, PhD, *Daring Greatly: How the Courage to be Vulnerable Transforms the Way We Live, Love, Parent, and Lead* (New York, Avery), 2012.
- Susan Cain, *Quiet: The Power of Introverts in a World That Can't Stop Talking* (New York, Broadway Books), 2013.
- C. Hope Clark, *The Shy Writer Reborn: An Introverted Writer's Wake-up Call* (USA, FundsforWriters Publication), 2013.
- Sophia Dembling, *Introvert's Way: Living a Quiet Life in a Noisy World* (New York, Perigree Book), 2012.
- Jenn Granneman, Introvert, Dear website, https://introvertdear.com

- Gill Hasson, *Mindfulness: Be Mindful. Live in the Moment* (New York, Fall River Press), 2013.

- Norma T. Hollis, *Ten Steps to Authenticity: Creating a Rewarding and Satisfying Life* (Los Angeles, Rhythm of the Drum Publications), 2008.

- Anne Janzer, *Get the Word Out: Write a Book That Makes a Difference* (San Luis Obispo, CA, Cuesta Park Consulting), 2020.

- Jennifer B. Kahnweiler, PhD, *The Introverted Leader: Building on Your Quiet Strength* (Oakland, CA, Berrett-Koehler Publishers, Inc.), 2018.

- Jennifer B. Kahnweiler, PhD, *Creating Introvert-Friendly Workplaces: How to Unleash Everyone's Talent and Performance* (Oakland, CA, Berrett-Koehler Publishers, Inc.), 2020.

- Mari L. McCarthy, *Journaling Power: How to Create the Happy, Healthy Life You Want to Live* (USA, Hasmark Publishing), 2016.

- Kristin Neff, PhD, *Self-Compassion: The Proven Power of Being Kind to Yourself* (USA, HarperCollins books), 2011.

- Thea Orozco, *The Introvert's Guide to the Workplace: Concrete Strategies for Bosses and Employees to Thrive and Succeed* (New York, Skyhorse Publishing), 2020.

- Lauren Sapala, *Firefly Magic: Heart Powered Marketing for Highly Sensitive Writers* (USA, Lauren Sapala), 2018.

# ACKNOWLEDGEMENTS

I am honored to acknowledge the contributions of so many culminating in *The Corporate Introvert*. Each helped expand my vision and improve my thoughts.

To the countless teammates, co-workers, and managers I worked alongside during my thirty years at Shell Oil, your wisdom, patience, lessons, and stories are woven into my life and the pages of *The Corporate Introvert*. I especially want to acknowledge Craig Linington. Sometimes the best is truly saved for last. He recognized what I needed to excel more than I did. He provided me with space and time, encouragement and recognition. I cannot thank him enough.

**Writing Circle:** my heartfelt appreciation to the talented ladies of our Writing Circle who provided critique and support, not just for my developing manuscript, but for me personally during the entire writing journey: Margo Catts, Karen Hale, Jean Nunnally, Amanda Olson, and Ronarose Train.

**Beta Contributors:** my tremendous gratitude to the TCI Beta Contributors who provided abundant constructive challenge, suggestions, and support during early development of *The Corporate Introvert*. Many of their stories have been included in the chapters within: Jay Artale, Sara Bonario, Ebere Chimezie, Matt Kingsolver, Michelle Lax, Todd Miner, and Sharon Pastor.

**Editors:** special appreciation to Anne Janzer who gently yet wisely guided me to develop my thoughts into a cohesive and inviting manuscript. I also want to acknowledge the contributions of my copy editor, Laura Roberts, who sharpened the flow and professionalism of my writing.

Anne Janzer: www.annejanzer.com.

Laura Roberts Creative Services: laurarobertscreativeservices.com

**Graphic Designers:** Alexander von Ness and Slim Rijeka of Ness Graphica, my cover designer and interior designer, did a marvelous job converting my vision into the style that matches my words and purpose.

Ness Graphica: www.NessGraphica.com.

# AUTHOR BIO

### If I Knew Then What I Know Now

*"I have finally realized, to be happy I don't need to change myself, I just need to be myself." -Steve Friedman*

When I wrote my memoir, *In Search of Courage*, I realized that the common thread of introversion I thought was a curse all my life was actually a blessing. For years I wore a mask at work and coped with my stress by sacrificing my health and personal relationships. Now I embrace my own introversion as a toolkit to become a happier me.

My purpose is to help other introverts to accelerate their own journey to discover their strengths and how to apply them at home and at work. I seek to inspire others to overcome past obstacles and find joy, pride, and confidence in life.

I've retired from corporate America and enjoy sharing articles, books, quizzes, and resources through my website, BeyondIntroversion.com. I'm excited to combine my career experiences and my enthusiastic belief in all introverts through my new leadership book, *The Corporate Introvert: How to Lead and Thrive with Confidence.*

**Beyond Introversion**

Discover your strengths and embrace your best self!

It's time for us to stop hiding or feeling the victim.
It's time to feel confident about our authentic selves.
It's time to get our unique voices into the room.

**It's time to go
Beyond Introversion!**

www.BeyondIntroversion.com

*Offering weekly posts, quizzes, and resources for today's
introverts.*

Also by Steve Friedman

*In Search of Courage:
An Introvert's Story*

In his award-winning memoir, author Steve Friedman shares his struggles both at work and at home. His long path to overcome countless roadblocks is both "heart-wrenching and heartbreaking."

Learn more and buy your copy here:

https://www.beyondintroversion.com/courage

# Contact Me

I love to engage with fellow introverts and extroverts who love and work with them. Drop me a line with your comments and questions.

## Email:
BeyondIntroversion@gmail.com

## Facebook:
https://www.facebook.com/BeyondIntroversion

## LinkedIn:
https://www.linkedin.com/in/steve-friedman-1295a5a2

Made in the USA
Monee, IL
12 January 2024

51636236R00138